STUDIES IN JOSEPHSON SUPERCOMPUTER DESIGN

also: Workstation Tools for Design — Proceedings of the
2nd AHPGRE Symposium Interaction Electronics
and Computer Design

ISSUES IN JOSEPHSON
SUPERCOMPUTER DESIGN

STUDIES IN JOSEPHSON SUPERCOMPUTERS

Issues in Josephson Supercomputer Design — Proceedings of the
6th and 7th RIKEN Symposia on Josephson Electronics
Eds. E Goto and K F Loe

Forthcoming:

Quantum Flux Parametron — A Single Quantum Flux Superconducting
Logic Device
by W Hioe and E Goto

Other related titles published:

D C Flux Parametron — A New Approach to Josephson Junction Logic
by E Goto and K F Loe

Fluxoid Josephson Computer Technology — Proceedings of the
3rd, 4th and 5th RIKEN-ERATO Symposia
Eds. E Goto, T Soma and K F Loe

Studies in Josephson Supercomputers

ISSUES IN JOSEPHSON SUPERCOMPUTER DESIGN

Proceedings of the 6th and 7th RIKEN Symposia
on Josephson Electronics

Tokyo   23 March 1989
               23 March 1990

Editors

E. Goto

Department of Information Science, University of Tokyo
Goto Quantum Magneto Flux Logic Project, Research Development Corporation of Japan

K. F. Loe

Department of Information Systems and Computer Science
National University of Singapore

World Scientific
Singapore • New Jersey • London • Hong Kong

Published by

World Scientific Publishing Co. Pte. Ltd.
P O Box 128, Farrer Road, Singapore 9128
USA office: 687 Hartwell Street, Teaneck, NJ 07666
UK office: 73 Lynton Mead, Totteridge, London N20 8DH

ISSUES IN JOSEPHSON SUPERCOMPUTER DESIGN
— Proceedings of the 6th and 7th RIKEN Symposia on
Josephson Electronics

ISBN 981-02-0129-X

Printed in Singapore by JBW Printers & Binders Pte. Ltd.

HS

Preface

Quantum Flux Parametron (QFP) is a Josephson junction device which uses the polarities of a unit of quantum flux to represent a bit of binary information. The low power consumption and the inductive nature of signal transfer of Quantum Flux Parametron promise the realizability of a highly integrated Josephson supercomputer. The miniaturization and the inductively connected circuits pose new challenges and problems to the designers of such a computer system. In this volume we have collected five papers which provide the detailed illustrations of the essential problems in the design of Josephson supercomputers.

The essential problems include (i) the three-dimensional packaging problems in the highly integrated system, (ii) the detection of trapped magnetic quanta, (iii) the computation of three-dimensional inductance and (iv) the elimination or alleviation of various internal and external operational problems of Quantum Flux Parametron arising from the limitation of the current fabrication technology as well as the inherent problems of direct coupling of Quantum Flux Parametron.

The problem (i) is addressed in the paper "Basic Technology for Three-Dimensional Packaging", the problem (ii) is addressed in the papers "Gas Floating Method of Pick-up Coil for Detection of Flux Trapped in Superconductors" as well as "Magnetic Field Distribution Arising from a Trapped Fluxon", the problem (iii) is addressed in the paper "Three-Dimensional Inductance Calculation", and the problem (iv) is addressed in "QFP QFP Logic (QQL)".

Some of the basic background and related study of Josephson Supercomputer design based on Quantum Flux Parametron can be found in the series of books published by World Scientific Publishing. They are "DC Flux Parametron — A New Approach to Josephson Junction Logic" written by Goto, E. and Loe, K. F., "Fluxoid Josephson Computer Technology" edited by Goto, E., Soma, T. and Loe, K. F., as well as a forthcoming book "Quantum Flux Parametron — A Single Quantum Flux Superconducting Logic Device" written by Hioe, W. and Goto, E.

Goto, E. and Loe, K. F.
Dec 1, 1990

Contents

Basic Technology for Three-Dimensional Packaging

Ryotaro Kamikawai, Yutaka Harada, Mutsumi Hosoya

Willy Hioe, Yasuo Wada, Hideaki Nakane and Eiichi Goto

1. Introduction

To enhance the performance of ultrahigh-speed computer hardware, (1) logic elements must be speeded up and (2) they must be packaged more compactly. Regarding the packing density, for example, if logic signals are to be sent from one side of the CPU to the other within a single machine cycle, then the dimensions of the CPU must be correspondingly diminished. Such miniaturization will soon be beyond the capacity of today's silicon transistor- based hardware. The prevailing silicon technology dissipates a great deal of heat per unit volume and is fast approaching its theoretical limits in density of features and therefore also hardware performance. This accounts for the great interest in quantum flux parametrons (QFPs), which would easily satisfy the above requirements. In terms of speed, for example, 5-GHz logic operations have already been demonstrated[1], and much faster speeds are likely to be achieved in the near future. QFPs also offer advantages for more compact packaging, especially their low power consumption and capacity for transformer-connection (the ability to transmit signals without actual physical contact). Figure 1.1 shows a three-dimensional packaging scheme that exploits these advantages. Assuming a QFP per-circuit power consumption of 1 nW (at 10-GHz operation), then a million QFPs could be packed together and consume no more than 1 mW. Liquid helium would be adequate for cooling such cubic modules ranging from 1 to 2 cm^2 in size. Moreover, since the substrates needn't be in actual contact to transmit signals, connectors are unnecessary and much greater densities can be achieved.

There are significant technological hurdles still to be overcome before this three-dimensional packaging approach can be implemented. For example, key requirements include:

(1) high-yield production of wafers on which QFP circuits are fabricated;

(2) a means of passing multiple signals through wafers from the front surface to the back surface; and

(3) a means of precisely aligning multiple wafers and interconnecting them.

Our research group is currently building a basic model to demonstrate the feasibility of the proposed three- dimensional packaging method. As shown in Fig. 1.2, the model consists of silicon chips mounted on a silicon wiring substrate.[2] As can be seen in the figure, QFP circuits are fabricated on a chip, activation lines to drive the QFP circuits are fabricated on the wiring substrate, and transformers (that do not require actual physical contact) are formed on chip and substrate to provide QFP-to-QFP interconnection. This approach dose not need requirements (1) and (2). Moreover, as to requirement (3), all that is needed is a technique of aligning two silicon pieces. With this prototype, we can demonstrate one of the key advantages of QFPs-the ability to interconnect them with transformer coupling that does not require physical contact.

2. Signal Transfer by Transformer

2.1 Transformer Parameters

Two types of transformers are required to implement our basic model: activation transformers to supply the activation signal, and I/O transformers to provide interconnection between the QFP circuits. The I/O transformer in particular must be carefully engineered to satisfy critical parameters that will be detailed in this section.

Output current from a QFP is greatest when the overall load inductance on connected I/O lines is given by

$$\pi L_Q / 2, \tag{1}$$

where L_Q is the equivalent inductance of the QFP, and this condition should be incorporated in the design[3].

If the same load (including a transformer) is imposed on n (implemented in parallel) lines as shown in Fig. 2.1, then the inductance for each line should be given by

$$n\pi L_Q/2. \tag{2}$$

The larger n is made, the more fanouts are available, but if the supply current to the next-stage QFP is reduced by too much, this could cause the circuit to fail[3]. In our current basic circuit, n = 4 (one transformer, one previous-stage QFP and a fanout of 2). To enable a larger fanout, we have developed a booster circuit, but this is described elsewhere[4]. Since $L_Q = 6.35$ pH for the process technology employed, this means the load inductance for each line is 40 pH.

The transformers and the next stage loads are shown in detail in Fig. 2.2. Transformer inductance consists of shunt and leakage, and can be represented as a T-type equivalent circuit. Transformers are also implemented on the receiving end of each fanout lead. The shunt inductance of the receiving-end transformers and the loads beyond the next-stage QFP are large compared to the QFP equivalent inductances placed in parallel, and can be neglected.

Transformer shunt inductance L_S and leakage inductance L_L are determined as follows.

(1) L_S is set to 40 pH. This is the inductance per load, as was shown above. Here, the effect of L_L is neglected because it is small compared to L_S.

(2) L_L is derived from the same condition that the per- load inductance (including wiring, receiving-end transformers, and next-stage QFP) = 40 pH (refer to Fig. 2.2). Thus,

$$L_T + 2L_L + L_Q = 40, \quad \text{[pH]} \tag{3}$$

where L_T is the wiring inductance. Substituting 6.35 pH for L_Q,

$$L_T + 2L_L = 34. \quad \text{[pH]} \tag{4}$$

Thus, L_L must be determined in relation to L_T. In the next section, we will describe a transformer configuration in relation to these actual inductance values.

2.2 Transformer Configuration

To achieve the necessary mutual inductance (i.e., L_S) with the smallest possible dimensions requires a transformer configuration with holes in the ground plane. Isolated holes through the superconductor, however, would result in fluxoids being trapped upon cooling, a result that would adversely impact the operation of the circuit. To prevent this from happening, the ground plane has been divided up into island regions surrounded by open spaces (called canals) as shown in (Fig. 2.3). The various symbols used in the following, representing the dimensions of the device are shown in Fig. 2.4.

L_S is determined by the size of the hole surrounded by windings and ground plane. A program for calculating inductances from three-dimensional conductor geometry [5] was used to determine the dependence of d, the distance around the periphery of the hole. The numerical calculation results are presented in Fig. 2.5. In the figure, g represents the distance between the primary winding and the secondary winding. For the calculation range, it is found that the transformer's shunt inductance can be well approximated by

$$L_S = 1.25 \ \mu_o d. \tag{5}$$

Since we already determined in Section 2.1 that $L_S = 40$ pH, an appropriate dimension for d is

$$d = 25 \ \mu m. \tag{6}$$

Transformer leakage inductance, L_L, on the other hand, can be approximated by

$$L_L = 1.25 \ \frac{\pi \mu_o g}{\ln r}. \tag{7}$$

These approximations (the curves) are shown together with results obtained by numerical calculation (point symbols) in Fig. 2.6. Separation g must be made 1.5 μm considering the fabrication process, and r must be 3.0 for reasons of practicality, therefore,

$$L_L = 6.7. \qquad [\text{pH}] \tag{8}$$

Referring to equation (4) preceding section, permissible wire inductance is

$$L_T = 20. \qquad [\text{pH}] \tag{9}$$

3. Package Assembly Technology

In order to actually construct the basic model described in the preceding sections, new technologies had to be developed to accurately align the chip over the substrate. This section provides an overview of these developments.

3.1 Process Steps

The general approach is illustrated in Fig. 3.1. The chip and substrate are bonded face-to-face; that is, with their fabricated circuitry facing inward toward each other. The chip is correctly positioned over the substrate with the aid of alignment marks inscribed on the back of the chip, then pressure is applied to bond the two elements together. To achieve this, process steps as illustrated in Figs. 3.2(1)-(4) are employed in addition to conventional circuit fabrication processes. Those steps are summarized below.

(1) Inscribe alignment marks on the back of the chip

With a commercially available double-sided aligner, inscribe alignment marks on the back on the chip (refer to Fig. 3.1). The procedure is shown in detail in Fig. 3.3.

(2) Inscribe alignment marks on the surface of the substrate

In a similar manner, inscribe alignment marks on the front surface of the substrate. This step is integrated with the regular substrate fabrication steps.

(3) Substrate-chip alignment

Making use of the alignment marks, bring chip and substrate into precise alignment. To realize the degree of precision needed, a new assembly system is being developed that will be described in the next section.

(4) Bonding

Once the die is in proper alignment over the substrate, proceed with bonding at the temperature and pressure prescribed. The adhesive to be used for the bonding must satisfy three fundamental criteria: it must provide good even coverage, it must withstand temperatures ranging from liquid helium to room temperature, and it must be free of dust particles and contaminants. Through preliminary testing, we determined that AZ-photo resist and epoxy- type adhesives satisfy all these requirements.

Through the complete sequence of steps (1)-(4), we have sought to achieve an overall horizontal alignment accuracy on the order of ± 5 μm (equivalent to the narrowest circuit line width).

3.2 Assembly System

No available system has the assembly capabilities we need: bringing chip and substrate into alignment as shown in Fig. 3.1, and performing the bonding with proper temperature and pressure. The main functional requirements are:

(1) Horizontal alignment accuracy: ±3 μm

(2) Target chip size: 2 mm × 5 mm to 3 mm × 5 mm

(3) Target substrate size: 5 mm × 7.5 mm to 10 mm × 20 mm

(4) Minimum space between on-board chips: 0.1 mm

(5) Thickness of chip and substrate: 470 μm (±20 μm)

(6) Temperature control: room temperature to 80°C in the central part of the substrate support

(7) Package assembly pressure: 10-300 g

A system with these various capabilities must incorporate a:

(a) horizontal movement mechanism to bring the chip and substrate into alignment;

(b) microscope and display to monitor horizontal adjustment to bring the chip and substrate into alignment;

(c) mechanism to adjust the microscope up and down to focus it;

(d) mechanism to apply the proper pressure to achieve bonding; and

(e) mechanism to control the temperature during bonding.

A conceptual schematic of the system is shown in Fig. 3.4. Requirement (b) is especially difficult to realize. Since the alignment marks on the substrate and on the back of the chip are separated by the thickness of the chip (about 500 μm), the microscope can't focus on both planes at the same time. Yet for alignment, two sets of marks have to appear together on the screen. Hitachi's Central Research Laboratory is currently working on a solution. The system will be fully described on another occasion.

4. Conclusions

The main points of this report are summarized as follows:

(1) We are developing a high-density three-dimensional packaging technology for application to ultrahigh-speed computers. To demonstrate the feasibility of QFP-to-QFP signal transmission by transformer coupling(without actual physical contact) we are building a prototype basic package module.

(2) In our model, output from an on-chip QFP is passed to the metallization on the substrate by transformers and then on to other QFPs.

(3) New transformers have been designed to take full advantage of the special properties of QFP circuits: open areas between ground planes (termed, *canals*) form 25-by-25-μm holes. Then, primary and secondary windings are sandwiched between the two ground-plane layers.

(4) To construct the basic model, a new assembly method has been developed that involves precise alignment between chip and substrate by inscribing alignment marks on the back of the former and on the front of the latter.

References

1. Y. Harada, et al., "QFP High-Speed Operation Experimental Results," RIKEN Symposium 1989, pp. 41-53.

2. Y. Harada, et al., "Proposed Packaging Method for QFPs," RIKEN Symposium 1989, pp. 54-70.

3. E. Goto, et al., "Fluxoid Josephson Computer," World Scientific, 1988.

4. W. Hioe, et al., "QFP-QFP Logic (QQL)," RIKEN Symposium 1989, pp. 32-53.

5. M. Hosoya, et al., "Inductance Calculation System for Superconducting Circuits," IEEE Trans. Magnetics, Vol. 25, No. 2, pp. 1111-1114, March 1989.

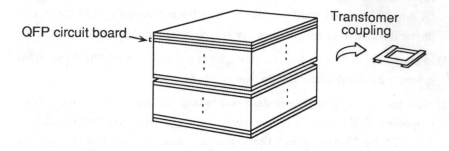

QFP circuit board

Transfomer coupling

Fig. 1.1 Three-dimensional packaging scheme

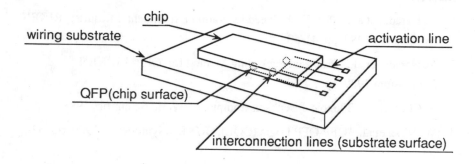

chip

wiring substrate

activation line

QFP(chip surface)

interconnection lines (substrate surface)

Fig. 1.2 Basic model

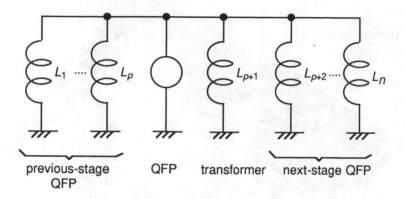

Fig. 2.1 QFP load

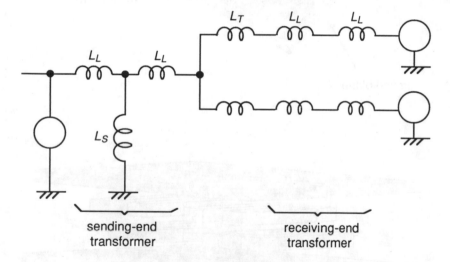

L_S : transformer shunt inductance
L_L : transformer leakage inductance
L_T : line inductance

Fig. 2.2 Details of QFP load (with fanout of 2)

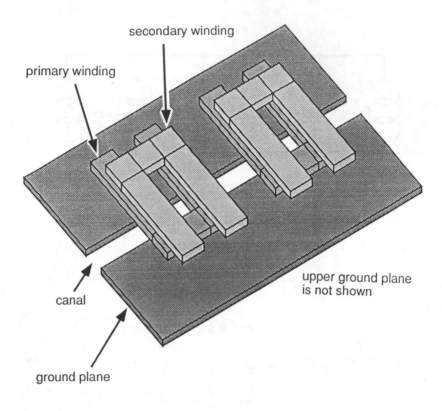

secondary winding

primary winding

canal

upper ground plane
is not shown

ground plane

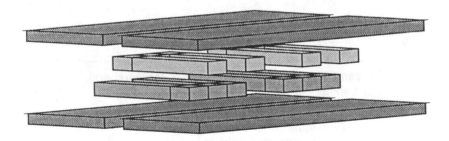

Fig. 2.3 Transformer configuration

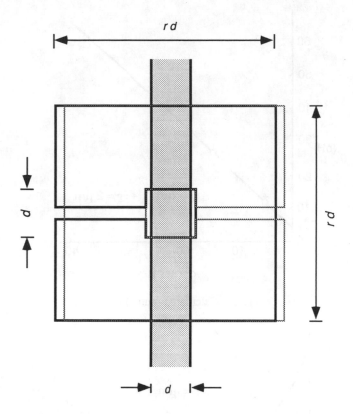

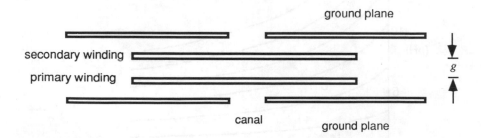

Fig. 2.4 Symbols of transformer dimensions

12

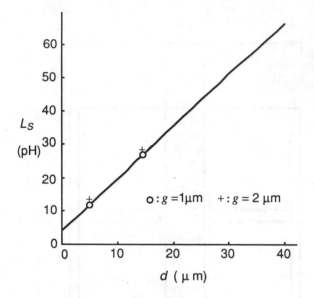

Fig. 2.5 Calculated mutual inductance

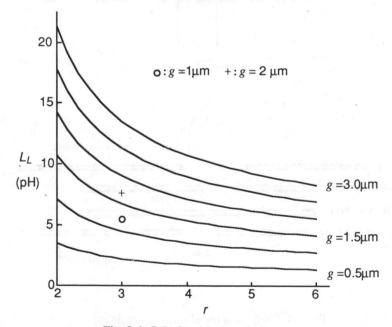

Fig. 2.6 Calculated leakage inductance

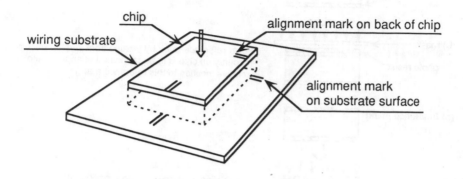

Fig.3.1 General approach of assembly

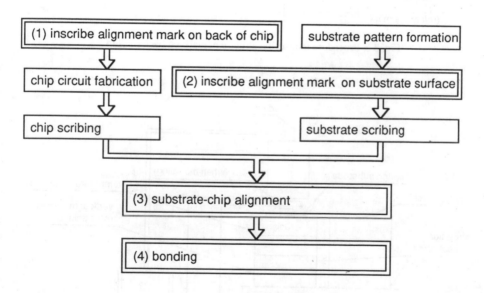

Fig. 3.2 Basic model process steps

14

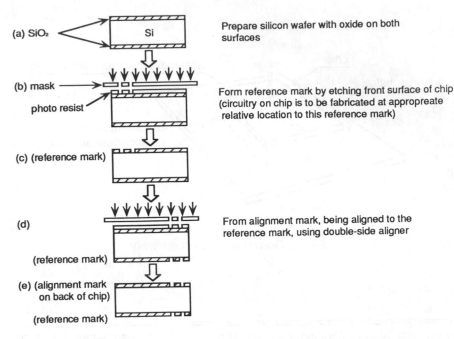

(a) SiO₂ — Prepare silicon wafer with oxide on both surfaces

Si

(b) mask —→

photo resist — Form reference mark by etching front surface of chip (circuitry on chip is to be fabricated at appropreate relative location to this reference mark)

(c) (reference mark)

(d) From alignment mark, being aligned to the reference mark, using double-side aligner

(reference mark)

(e) (alignment mark on back of chip)

(reference mark)

Fig. 3-3 Procedure to inscribe alignment mark on back of chip

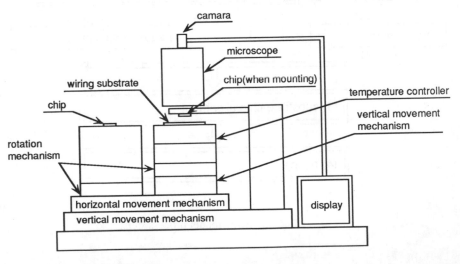

camara
microscope
wiring substrate
chip(when mounting)
temperature controller
chip
vertical movement mechanism
rotation mechanism
horizontal movement mechanism
display
vertical movement mechanism

Fig. 3-4 Corceptual schematic of assembly system

Gas Floating Method of Pick-up Coil for Detection of Flux Trapped in Superconductors

Hirofumi Minami, Qiquan Geng, Kazunori Chihara,

Junpei Yuyama and Eiichi Goto

Abstract

In the previous report, a theory concerning the floating height (gap spacing between the head and the sample) of a gas floating head was proposed, and it was reported that the relationship between the floating height and the pressure of the supplied gas was fully explained by the theoretical formula. However, the relationship between the floating height and the gas flow rate was not sufficiently explained. Thus in this report, our theoretical model is modified, introducing an empirical coefficient, for the purpose of considering axial symmetry and non-uniformity in the velocity. The agreement between the measured and theoretical values for the relationship between the floating height and flow rate was improved, and the floating height in liquid nitrogen could be qualitatively explained. Furthermore, in liquid helium, using a pick-up coil mounted on the gas floating head, the magnetic field distribution above the surface of a superconducting sample was measured. The change in magnetic field over the surface was observed. This change can be considered to be due to the trapped flux in the sample.

1. Introduction

There are several requirements for accurate measurement of the distribution of the trapped flux in a superconducting sample using the pick-up coil of a SQUID magnetometer. They are 1) bringing the coil as close as possible to the source of the magnetic flux so as to improve the signal-to-noise ratio and spatial resolution, 2) keeping a fixed distance between the coil and sample (variation in this distance produces fluctuation in the output, 3) stable scanning without the coil coming in contact with the sample, and 4) being usable in liquid helium (4.2K). The gas floating head is devised as a means of satisfying these requirements. At a fixed gas supply pressure, if the head moves away from the sample, an attractive force resulting from the action of the gas flow operates; if the head moves closer to the sample, then a repulsive force operates. Then the head floats stably at the balance point between the two opposing forces (attractive force equals repulsive force). This point is the floating height.

In the previous report (6th RIKEN Symposium),[2] data from room-temperature experiments revealed that the head will float at the balance point between the repulsive and attractive forces, and that the floating height could be controlled by varying the gas supply pressure. It was also reported that the relationship between the floating height and gas pressure within our experimental range could be sufficiently explained by our model based on the boundary layer theory.

In this report, we attempt to improve the description of the relationship between the gas flow rate and floating height, which was not sufficiently explained by the approximate equation used previously. Thus, we begin with a description of that approximate equation. Next, the results of an experiment in which the floating height was measured in liquid nitrogen are presented. Finally, we describe the results of an attempt to measure the magnetic field distribution above a superconducting sample in liquid helium with a pick-up coil mounted on the gas floating head.

2. Improvement of the Gas Floating Head Theory

2.1 Improved points

In the last report, within the gap formed by the head surface and the sample surface, and using only the distance x from the gas nozzle of the head, displacement thickness δ (a measure of thickness of the boundary layer appearing on both sides) was defined as

$$\delta(x) = 1.721 \times \frac{0.569}{0.648} \left(\frac{\mu x}{\rho U_m} \right)^{1/2} \tag{1}$$

where μ is a fluid viscosity, ρ is fluid density, and U_m is fluid velocity at the middle point between the gap entrance and exit. With the method from the last report, which used Eq. (1), the calculated values agreed well with the measured values for the relationship between the floating height and the gas supply pressure. However, the relationship between the floating height and the gas flow rate was not sufficiently explained. To improve the explanation, in this report an empirical coefficient α is introduced to replace the factor $(0.569/0.648)$ used in Eq. (1) to reflect axial symmetry. The displacement thickness δ is thus now defined as

$$\delta(x)=1.721 \times \alpha \times \left(\frac{\mu x}{\rho U}\right)^{1/2} \qquad (2)$$

If in Eq. (2) α is set to 1.0, the equation is in agreement with an expression of the displacement thickness of a boundary layer above a flat plate placed parallel to the flow. The coefficient α represents the following effects.

(1) Axial symmetry of the flow: if the analytically determined displacement thickness for the planar flow around the stagnation point and that for the axially symmetrical flow around the stagnation point are compared, it is seen that the displacement thickness of the axially symmetrical flow is smaller. The ratio of these two values is the constant (0.569/0.648) used in Eq. (1). However, this ratio for the flow in the gap between the head and sample cannot be guaranteed to be the same as for the flow in the vicinity of the stagnation point, so in this report the axial symmetry effect is included in the coefficient α.

(2) Radial change of the flow velocity: For planar flow, the flow velocity outside the boundary layer is constant (U). However, in the case of the gas floating head, the flow velocity outside the boundary layer decreases as the flow proceeds from the nozzle towards the outside of the head, because of the increasing circumference of the flow area. On the other hand, it is known that, if the flow rate U is expressed in terms of a power of x, the displacement thickness is obtained analytically and the coefficient 1.721 is altered according to the exponent. Thus, in this report flow rate U is represented by the flow rate at the midpoint between the gap entrance and exit, denoted by U_m, and the change in the coefficient due to velocity change is taken into account in α.

2.2 Calculation method

In the last report, the flow coefficient C_o (which represents the ratio of the effective cross-sectional area narrowed by the curvature of the flow lines to the geometrical cross-sectional area at the entrance of the gap) was used, and its value was determined so as to produce a good fit between the calculated values and the measured values. In the present study, the coefficient α described in section 2.1 is not obtained theoretically, so we chose to determine it empirically together with the C_o coefficient used in the last report. In the experiment, the floating height and flow rate were obtained for a given gas supply pressure. Thus, by optimizing the two values (C_o and α), the calculated values for both the floating height and the flow rate were made to approach the measured values. To evaluate the degree of agreement between the measured and calculated values, the standard deviations (σ_h and σ_Q) of the two values were used. Also, in the present calculations, gas supply pressures (the value after correction for pressure drop in the gas supply tube) of 800 Torr or more were used for the following reasons.

(1) Above 800 Torr, there are experimental advantages in that there is little fluctuation in floating height, even if there is fluctuation in the gas supply pressure, and because rigidity related to the floating height is high, the floating height is stable even if some small external force is applied.

(2) Below 800 Torr, there is large change in the floating height and flow rate with the gas supply pressure. Thus, pressure measurement error (including pressure drop correction) results in a large error in floating height and flow rate.

2.3 Comparison of measured and theoretical values

Using the calculation method of section 2.2 to find the combination of C_o and α which simultaneously minimizes the standard deviation of the floating height, σ_h, and the standard deviation of the flow rate, σ_Q, we obtain $C_o = 0.90$ and $\alpha = 0.77$. These values result in the standard deviations of $\sigma_h = 2.73$ μm and $\sigma_Q = 0.94$ SLM.

The measured and calculated values for floating height and gas supply pressure are compared in Fig. 1. In the figure, two sets of experimental data are presented. The second data set is from a repetition of the experiment after the equipment had been disassembled and then reassembled. The purpose of this was to avoid systematic errors such as those due to differences in positioning of the equipment during assembly. From the viewpoint of fluid action, this should be considered as a single experiment, so σ_h and σ_Q are obtained using both sets of data. The measured and calculated values for floating height and gas flow rate are compared in Fig. 2. From this figure, we can see that the agreement between theoretical and experimental values for the relationship between the floating height and gas flow rate was improved in comparison with the previous values (theoretical curve shown with C_o=1.00, α=0.88)

2.4 Results

The problem was studied again by introducing the empirical coefficient α and using it together with the empirically obtained flow coefficient C_o. At C_o= 0.90 and α = 0.77, the agreement between theoretical and measured values for the relationship between the floating height and flow rate was improved.

3. Gas Floating Head in Liquid Nitrogen and Liquid Helium

In the present study, gas was supplied to the gas floating head in liquid nitrogen, and the relation between floating height and flow rate and changes in floating height during sample rotation were measured. In the experiment, aluminum electrodes were attached to the surfaces of the head and sample, and changes in the capacitance were measured with a capacitance bridge.

3.1 Measurement of the floating height

The head used in the floating height measurements was the same head used in the previous room-temperature measurements, with an electrode attached. The supplied gas was nitrogen. The relationship between the measured floating heights and the gas flow rate is shown in Fig. 3. As the flow rate is increased from 0 up to 20 SLM, the floating height increased to about 320 µm. Here the floating height becomes small suddenly and it becomes stable at a height of about 70 µm with a flow rate of 20 SLM or more. The behavior in the flow rate region of 20 SLM or more is qualitatively the same as the results obtained at room temperature. However, the results are different below 20 SLM. The reasons for this behavior of the head in liquid nitrogen are now being investigated.

The flow rate data in the region of 20 SLM or more is compared in Fig. 4 with the theoretical values obtained with the formula explained earlier. In the figure, the measured values are indicated by open circles (O) and the solid line represents the theoretical values determined by $C_o = 0.80$ and $\alpha = 1.08$. However, in the theoretical values the flow velocity within the gap becomes very large if flow rate exceeds 22 SLM, and cannot be analyzed by our model. Thus, values above 22 SLM are not plotted here. The values used here for C_o and α are different from the values used in the room-temperature experiment ($C_o = 0.90$ and $\alpha = 0.77$) because the dimensions of the heads used in the two experiments were different. In the room temperature experiment, the outer diameter of the head was 16 mm and the diameter of the nozzle was 4 mm. However, the respective dimensions of the head used at liquid nitrogen temperatures were 24 mm and 4 mm. (The diameter was increased for the purpose of connecting lead wires to the electrode.) This difference in the size of the head surface is thought to affect the values of C_o and α.

In this way, by selecting appropriate values for C_o and α, our theoretical formula is able to qualitatively explain the data measured at liquid nitrogen temperatures within a certain region. (As shown in Fig. 3, the experimentally measured behavior of the head differs in the regions above and below the flow rate of 20 SLM. Also, as explained above, the theoretical formula used in the present study cannot be used in the region above 22 SLM. Thus the region in which measured and theoretical results can be compared is small.)

3.2 Change in floating height during sample rotation

Stability in floating height during sample rotation was measured. A head, which is supported by three thin pipes with an outer diameter of 0.5 mm and inner diameter of 0.4 mm, was used for this measurement. These pipes also are used to supply the gas for the gas floating head. In the measurement procedure, first the head is placed in contact with the sample, with no gas supplied. Next, gas is supplied, floating the head. The sample is then rotated, and change in the capacitance is measured. The rotation was limited to from 0° to 100° because of the lead wires connected to the electrodes. At a helium gas flow rate of 33 NLM, the fractional change in the floating height (change in floating height divided by the average floating height) accompanying the sample rotation was approximately ±10%.

3.3 Results

The experiment on floatation in liquid nitrogen showed that a flow rate of 20 SLM or more produces a floating height of about 70 μm. It also revealed that our theoretical formula can explain the experimental data qualitatively to a certain extent, even at liquid nitrogen temperatures. Finally, it was determined that the fractional change in floating height accompanying sample rotation was approximately ±10% in liquid helium.

4. Measurement of the Magnetic Field distribution

We attempted to measure the magnetic field distribution over a superconducting sample in liquid helium, using a pick-up coil mounted on the gas floating head. The superconducting sample was a niobium film (1.3 μm thick) formed on half the surface of a 2-inch silicon substrate. The purpose of this was to allow a comparison of the niobium-covered surface with the uncovered surface in the experiments.

4.1 Vibration of the head during gas supply

The head with coil attached and the sample were placed inside the lead enclosure in a helium Dewar. This cryostat was then inserted into three Premalloy shields.

The noise level of the SQUID magnetometer was measured using a spectrum analyzer. The results showed that when gas was not supplied, the noise level was $4 \times 10^{-4} \phi_0/\sqrt{Hz}$ and the noise level did not change, even when helium gas was supplied at a flow rate of 50 LM. Thus, the increase in noise level is less than the system noise, so the vibration of the head by supplied gas gives no problem to the measurement at this stage.

4.2 SQUID magnetometer output during sample rotation

The SQUID magnetometer output when the sample was rotated at 1 rpm while helium gas was supplied at a flow rate of 35 LM is shown in Fig. 5 for (1) clockwise rotation, and (2) counterclockwise rotation. From the figure we can see a periodic signal with the sample rotation. The signal is smooth in a half cycle, and the signal has steep peaks and valleys in the other half cycle. There is symmetry in the output for the two opposite directions of rotation.

4.3 Change after a heat cycle

The change after a heat cycle is shown in Fig. 6. This data was obtained by returning the cryostat to room temperature after the first run (the measurements shown in Fig. 5), and then once again cooling down to liquid helium temperatures and repeating the experiment. To make the trapped flux small in the second run, the cooling was done by making the immersion into the liquid helium as slow as possible (1 mm/min.). The data for the first run is shown in Fig. 6-(1) and for the second in fig. 6-(2). These field measurements were made at the same position on the same sample. Fig. 6-(3) shows the background magnetic field in the cryostat. This signal was got after getting the Fig. 6-(2) signal with the sample removed from the sample folder while the cryostat were kept in liquid helium. From Fig. 6, we can see a smooth output in a half cycles (Part A), where only the background magnetic field in the cryostat is detected, and steep peaks and valleys in the other half cycles (Part B), where the magnetic field distribution above the surface of a niobium film is detected. These peaks and valleys are thought to arise from trapped flux in the niobium film.

4.4 Distribution of the magnetic field on the sample surface

Magnetic field distribution arising from the superconducting sample is shown on Fig. 7. This is obtained by using the data obtained in the second run (described above). The output signal in which the sample is removed is subtracted from the output signal in which the sample is present. From this figure, we see that in the half-cycle where the niobium film is not present, there is nearly constant output signal. In the half-cycle in which the niobium film is present, the magnetic field distribution shows steep variation because of the influence of trapped flux in the niobium film. At the edge of the niobium film, we can see a intense magnetic field because of demagnetizing effect of the superconductor.

4.5 Results

The system noise of the SQUID magnetometer, including the pick-up coil mounted on the head, is $4 \times 10^{-4}\ \phi_0/\sqrt{Hz}$, and we can see no change in the noise level when gas is supplied. The output of the SQUID magnetometer is symmetrical with respect to clockwise rotation and counterclockwise rotation of the sample. The signal in Part B changed after warming up to room temperature and then cooling down to liquid helium temperature. This suggests that the signal in Part B relates to the superconducting film.

5. Summary

1. Our theoretical model based on the boundary-layer theory is improved by introducing a new empirical coefficient. The result was an improvement in the agreement of the theoretically predicted values and the experimentally measured values for the relationship between the floating height and the gas flow rate (for the room temperature experiments).

2. Head floatation experiments carried out in liquid nitrogen showed that the head floated at a height of about 70 μm. It was also revealed that the theoretical formula can qualitatively explain the experimental results even at liquid nitrogen temperatures.

3. In liquid helium, a SQUID magnetometer with a pick-up coil supported by the gas floatation method was used to measure the magnetic field distribution above the surface of a superconducting sample. The magnetic field distribution arising from in trapped flux in the superconductor was measured.

Acknowledgement

We wish to express our deep gratitude to Humio Naruse, ULVAC JAPAN Ltd., for much advice concerning the theoretical analysis.

References

1. J. Yuyama, E. Goto, Proceedings of the 4th RIKEN Symposium on Josephson Electronics, pp.91-101, 1987, Fluxoid Josephson Computer Technology (E.

Goto, T. Soma, and K.F. Loe, Eds.), World Scientific, Singapore, pp.24-34, 1988.

2. H. Minami, J. Yuyama, E. Goto, and H . Naruse, 6th RIKEN Symposium on Josephson Electronics, pp.89-101, 1989.

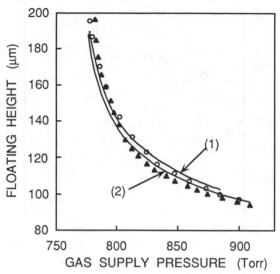

Fig. 1 Comparison of the experimental and theoretical values for floating height and gas supply pressure at room temperature. Supply gas is air. The theoretical values are shown with solid curve (1) ($C_0=1.00$, $\alpha=0.80$) and solid curve (2) ($C_0=0.90$, $\alpha=0.77$).. Two sets of experimental data are shown with symbol ▲ and symbol ○ .

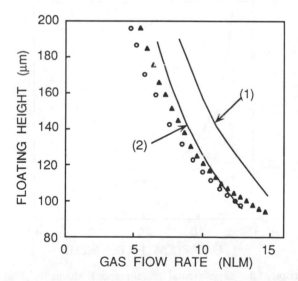

Fig. 2 Comparison of the experimental and theoretical values for floating height and gas flow rate at room temperature. Conition is same as figure 1.

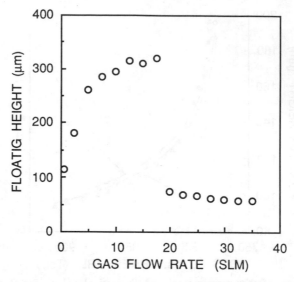

Fig. 3   The relationship between the measured floating height and gas flow rate
in liquid Nitrogen.

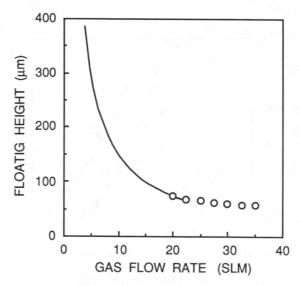

Fig. 4   Comparison of the experimental and theoretical values for floating height
and gas flow rate in liquid Nitrogen. The theoretical and the measured
values are indicated by solid curve and open circles respectively.

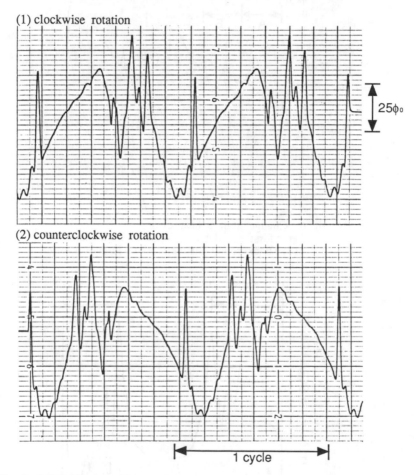

Fig. 5 SQUID magnetometer output when the sample was rotated at 1 rpm
while herium gas was supplied at a flow rate of 35LM.

28

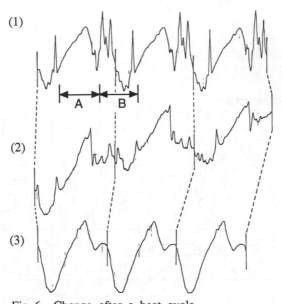

Fig. 6   Change after a heat cycle.
(1) : First run data.   (2) : Second run data.
(3) : Background magnetic field in the cryostat.

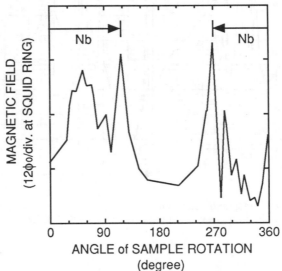

Fig. 7   Distribution of the magnetic field on the sample surface.

Magnetic Field Distribution Arising from a Trapped Fluxon

Qiquan Geng and Eiichi Goto

Abstract

Simple model calculations have been performed in relation to the potential and the magnetic field distribution produced by a trapped fluxon in thin superconducting films, aiming at the detection of the flux quantum by SQUID.

1. Introduction

Information concerning the distribution of magnetic flux quanta on superconducting films is of importance for achieving perfect magnetic shielding/1,2/. Furthermore, trapped magnetic flux quanta in Josephson electric circuits cause serious problems for the operation of these devices/3,4/. Therefore, the detection of a single trapped fluxon is strongly needed. In a large thin superconducting film, direct observation of single trapped fluxon has been reported/5/. However, it is still a question that how to detect a fluxon trapped in a superconducting strip sample by SQUID, or more specifically, how to trace out the distribution of the trapped fluxons from the detected SQUID signal. Recently we have attempted to answer such question. This report presents the part of which effort.

2. Infinite large superconducting thin film and monopole model

Let's consider a large superconducting thin film. Since the radius of trapped flux (order of penetration depth $\lambda \approx 0.05$ μm), is much much smaller than the dimension of the film, this plane can be regarded as an infinite one. To such problem, we use monopole model for a first approximation. Thus, in cylindrical coordinate (z, R, ϕ), the magnetic potential:

$$\Phi(z,R) = \frac{\Phi_0}{2\pi \ (\ z^2 + R^2 \ )^{1/2}} \tag{2.1}$$

and the z component of magnetic field:

$$B_z(z,R) = -\frac{d\Phi}{dz} = \frac{\Phi_0 \, z}{2\pi(\, z^2 + R^2 \,)^{3/2}} \qquad (2.2)$$

where $\Phi_0 = 2.068$ fWb is the flux quantum or fluxon.

Once we know the magnetic field distribution in space, we can do a simple integration to estimate the signal that can be detected by SQUID pick-up coil.

At this point, one may request how good this monopole model could be. To check it, one of course need to apply Ginzburg-Landau theory to get an exactly solution. However, at a place where the distance ($z \approx 20$ μm) is much larger than λ, the monopole model should be well valid, since the affect of the generated superconducting current within the penetration depth is expected to be negligible small. Actually, if we neglect the generated superconducting current, we can solve such a problem by using Green function to get same results as monopole model (Appendix Eqs.(A.10) and (A.11)). Furthermore, Eq.(2.1) suggests that the flux line fan out from the trapped isolated flux center, which is consistent with the previous observation/5/.

3. Superconducting strip line

In this situation, the problem becomes more complicated, since the dimension of strip line (order of tens micrometer) could be much smaller than the diameter of pick-up coil and maybe in the same order of pick-up coil wires. Fortunately, all those dimensions are much larger than 0.05 μm (the order of penetration depth), thus we can use the monopole model to calculate the distribution of magnetic potential and discuss the effects of pick-up coil dimension afterwards.

Let us now consider more symmetrical case: A fluxon Φ_0 is trapped at the center of a superconducting circle (located at $z = 0$ plane with radius of 1), then free space outside, or in other words, $\Phi = $ constant $= 0$ when $z = 0$ and $R > 1$ in cylindrical coordinate.

To such a problem, we use oblate spheroidal coordinates (σ, τ, ϕ). First let's assume that there are some magnetic charges inside a hole (radius of 1), then the upper part space solution will be

$$\Phi = S_n(\sigma) \, T_n(\tau) . \qquad (3.1)$$

Substituting Eq(3.1) into Laplace equation

$$\nabla^2 \Phi = 0 , \tag{3.2}$$

we obtain

$$\nabla^2 \Phi = \sum_{n=0}^{\infty} \left[\frac{\partial}{\partial \sigma} [(1+\sigma^2) \frac{\partial S_n(\sigma)}{\partial \sigma}] T_n(\tau) + \frac{\partial}{\partial \tau} [(1-\tau^2) \frac{\partial T_n(\tau)}{\partial \tau}] S_n(\sigma) \right]$$

$$= 0 . \tag{3.3}$$

By using standard variable separation method and replacing σ roman with $i\,\sigma$, we have

$$\begin{cases} \frac{\partial}{\partial \tau} \left[(1-\tau^2) \frac{\partial T_n(\tau)}{\partial \tau} \right] + n(n+1)\, T_n(\tau) = 0 \\[4mm] \frac{\partial}{\partial \sigma} \left[(1-\sigma^2) \frac{\partial S_n^*(\sigma)}{\partial \sigma} \right] + n(n+1)\, S_n^*(\sigma) = 0 \end{cases} \tag{3.4}$$

where $S_n^*(\sigma) = S_n(i\,\sigma)$.

Eq.(3.4) is typical Legendre equation. Its solution is

$$\Phi = \sum_{n=0}^{\infty} \left[a_n\, (Q_n^*(\sigma)+c_n\, P_n^*(\sigma))\, P_n(\tau) + b_n\, (Q_n^*(\sigma)+c_n\, P_n^*(\sigma))\, Q_n(\tau) \right]$$

$$\tag{3.5}$$

with

$$\begin{cases} P_n(x) = \frac{1}{2^n n!} \frac{d^n}{dx^n} (x^2-1)^n \\[4mm] Q_n(x) = \frac{1}{2^n n!} \frac{d^n}{dx^n} \left[(x^2-1)^n \ln\frac{1+x}{1-x} \right] - \frac{1}{2} P_n(x) \ln\frac{1+x}{1-x} \end{cases} \tag{3.6}$$

and

$$\begin{cases} P_n^*(\sigma) = \frac{P_n(i\,\sigma)}{i^n} \\[4mm] Q_n^*(\sigma) = \frac{Q_n(i\,\sigma)}{i^{n+1}} \end{cases} \tag{3.7}$$

with all terms are positive.

Now let us consider the boundary conditions.

a) Φ must be finite. Since on the z-axis

$$\lim_{\tau \to \pm 1} Q_n(\tau) \to \infty \qquad (3.8)$$

it leads

$$b_n \equiv 0. \qquad (3.9)$$

b)

$$\lim_{\sigma \to \infty} \Phi = \lim_{\sigma \to \infty} (Q_n^*(\sigma) + c_n P_n^*(\sigma)) = 0 \qquad (3.10)$$

leads

$$c_n \equiv -\frac{\pi}{2}. \qquad (3.11)$$

c)

$$\Phi(\tau=0) = 0 \qquad (3.12)$$

leads

$$a_{2n} \equiv 0. \qquad (3.13)$$

Thus we have

$$\Phi = \sum_{n=0}^{\infty} a_{2n+1} \; P_{2n+1}(\tau) \left[Q_{2n+1}^*(\sigma) - \frac{\pi}{2} P_{2n+1}^*(\sigma) \right] \qquad (3.14)$$

Let's come back to real situation: (i) only a point magnetic charge at origin; (ii) no charge inside the hole. Therefore the real magnetic potential is

$$\Phi_{tot} = \frac{1}{X} + \Phi_{cor} + \sum_{n=0}^{\infty} a_{2n+1} \; P_{2n+1}(\tau) \left[Q_{2n+1}^*(\sigma) - \frac{\pi}{2} P_{2n+1}^*(\sigma) \right]$$

$$(3.15)$$

where X is the distance between observation point and origin, and

$$\Phi_{cor} = \sum_{n=0}^{\infty} d_{2n+1} \left. \int_S \frac{q_{2n+1}(r)}{\sqrt{X^2 + r^2 - 2rX\cos\phi}} \, dS \right|_{\sigma=0} \qquad (3.16)$$

with $4\pi\varepsilon = 1$.

If we define

$$q_{2n+1}(r) \equiv \frac{P_{2n+1}(\tau)}{\tau} \quad , \qquad (3.17)$$

then boundary condition

$$\left. \frac{\partial\Phi_{tot}}{\partial z} \right|_{0<r\le1, z=0} = 0 \qquad (3.18)$$

leads

$$\begin{cases} d_1 = \dfrac{\pi}{2} a_1 \\[2mm] d_3 = \dfrac{3\pi}{4} a_3 \\[2mm] d_5 = \dfrac{15\pi}{16} a_5 \\[2mm] d_7 = \dfrac{35\pi}{32} a_7 \\[2mm] d_9 = \dfrac{315\pi}{256} a_9 \end{cases} \qquad (3.19)$$

Using Legendre expansion

$$\frac{1}{\sqrt{1 + s^2 - 2s\cos\theta}} = \sum_{m=0}^{\infty} p_m(\cos\theta)\, s^m \qquad (|s| < 1) \qquad (3.20)$$

we obtain

$$\Phi_{cor} = \sum_{n=0}^{\infty} U_{2n+1}(X) \qquad (3.21)$$

where

$$U_{2n+1}(X) = \sum_{m=0}^{\infty} \int_0^1 d_{2n+1}\, q_{2n+1}(r) \frac{r^{2m+1}}{X^{2m+1}}\, dr \times 2\pi\, P_{2m} \qquad (3.22)$$

34

and

$$P_m = \frac{1}{2\pi} \int_0^{2\pi} P_m(\cos\theta)\, d\theta$$

(3.23)

with

$$
\begin{cases}
P_{2m+1} \equiv 0 \\[4pt]
P_0 = 1 \\[4pt]
P_2 = \frac{1}{4} \\[4pt]
P_4 = \frac{9}{64} \\[4pt]
P_6 = \frac{25}{256} \\[4pt]
P_8 = \frac{35^2}{2^{14}}
\end{cases}
$$

(3.24)

Thus the boundary condition

$$\Phi_{tot}(\tau=0) = 0$$

(3.25)

becomes

$$\left[\frac{1}{X} + \sum_{n=0}^{\infty} U_{2n+1}(X) \right]_{X\geq 1, z=0} = 0$$

(3.26)

By considering first 4 terms, we obtain the matrix

$$
\begin{pmatrix}
\pi & -\frac{\pi}{4} & \frac{\pi}{8} & -\frac{5\pi}{64} \\[6pt]
\frac{1}{2} & -\frac{1}{3} & \frac{13}{96} & -\frac{13}{160} \\[6pt]
\frac{1}{3} & -\frac{7}{24} & \frac{19}{120} & -\frac{41}{480} \\[6pt]
\frac{1}{4} & -\frac{1}{4} & \frac{13}{80} & -\frac{13}{140}
\end{pmatrix}
\begin{pmatrix} d_1 \\ d_3 \\ d_5 \\ d_7 \end{pmatrix}
=
\begin{pmatrix} -1 \\ 0 \\ 0 \\ 0 \end{pmatrix}
$$

(3.27)

The solution of Eq.(3.27)

$$
\begin{cases}
d_1 = -\dfrac{32}{21\pi} \\[2mm]
d_3 = -\dfrac{112}{33\pi} \\[2mm]
d_5 = -\dfrac{1600}{273\pi} \\[2mm]
d_7 = -\dfrac{2240}{429\pi}
\end{cases}
\tag{3.28}
$$

and

$$
\begin{cases}
a_1 = -\dfrac{64}{21\pi^2} \\[2mm]
a_3 = -\dfrac{448}{99\pi^2} \\[2mm]
a_5 = -\dfrac{5120}{819\pi^2} \\[2mm]
a_7 = -\dfrac{2048}{429\pi^2}
\end{cases}
\tag{3.29}
$$

The approximation by considering only first 4 terms is

$$
\Phi_{tot}\Big|_{\tau=0,X\geq1} = \frac{35}{32}\frac{1}{1024}\frac{1}{X^9} \leq 10^{-3}
\tag{3.30}
$$

Therefore the magnetic potential produced by trapped fluxon in strip sample is

$$
\Phi_{tot} = \frac{1}{X} + \sum_{n=0}^{3} d_{2n+1} \int_S \frac{q_{2n+1}(r)}{\sqrt{X^2 + r^2 - 2rX\cos\phi}}\, dS \Bigg|_{\sigma=0}
$$

$$
+ \sum_{n=0}^{3} a_{2n+1} P_{2n+1}(\tau)\left[Q^*_{2n+1}(\sigma) - \frac{\pi}{2} P^*_{2n+1}(\sigma) \right]
\tag{3.31}
$$

with the coefficients given by Eqs.(3.28) and (3.29).

From Eq.(3.31), we can easily calculate the potential and the magnetic field at any point in upper space. For instance, after some mathematics manipulation, the potential and the magnetic field distributions at z=0 plane are

$$\Phi_{tot} = \begin{cases} \dfrac{1}{X} - \dfrac{64}{\pi^2}(1-X^2)^{\frac{3}{2}}\left[\dfrac{1}{3} - \dfrac{16}{15}(1-X^2) + \dfrac{32}{35}(1-X^2)^2\right] \\[2ex] \quad -8\sum_{n=0}^{4}P_{2n}(4n+1)\Bigg\{\left[\dfrac{2X}{(n+1)(2n-1)} - \dfrac{15X^3}{(n+2)(2n-3)} + \right. \\[2ex] \qquad\qquad \dfrac{30X^5}{(n+3)(2n-5)} - \dfrac{35X^7}{2(n+4)(2n-7)}\bigg] \\[2ex] \qquad\qquad -\left[\dfrac{4}{2n-1} - \dfrac{30}{2n-3} + \dfrac{60}{2n-5} - \dfrac{35}{2n-7}\right]X^{2n}\Bigg\} \\[2ex] \qquad\qquad\qquad (X < 1) \\[3ex] \dfrac{35}{32}\dfrac{1}{1024}X^{-9} \qquad\qquad\qquad\qquad (X > 1) \end{cases}$$

$$(3.32)$$

$$B_z = \frac{1}{\sigma}\frac{\partial\Phi}{\partial\tau}$$

$$= -\frac{8}{\pi^2}\left\{\left(\frac{\pi}{2} - \arctan\sigma\right)(1+15\sigma^2+45\sigma^4+35\sigma^6)-7\sigma-\frac{100}{3}\sigma^3-35\sigma^5\right\}$$

$$(3.33)$$

Their behaviors as a function of X or $\sigma = (X^2 - 1)^{1/2}$ are shown in Figure 1 and Figure 2 respectively. The approximation we made in the calculation is clearly indicated in Figure 1, which is not same as δ function. We expect that this error will be much smaller if we consider the higher terms, for instance 6 or 8 terms, in deducing Eq.(3.31).

4. Discussion

In principle, as mentioned in section 2, if no noise problem, one can obtain the flux which passed through a pick-up coil. An example is shown in Fig. 3. Where an one-loop coil with normalized radius of 20 is swept through the trapped fluxon at a constant height of 0.4 above the superconducting circle. The maximum signal change $\Delta\Phi$ is about 0.1 Φ_0, which is a fair large signal for the SQUID. However in the very narrow line strip experiments, the situation is very complicated. There are many sources that could distort the signal besides SQUID itself, such as (i) the superconducting current generated in penetration depth; (ii) the mutual inductance between superconductor and pick-up coil; (iii) the diameter of wire of the pick-up coil ($\approx$ 60 μm) is not negligible small; (iv) the distance between the pick-up coil and the superconducting strip can not be made infinite small i.e. z « 20 μm; (v) the diameter of the pick-up coil is neither infinite large nor infinite small, etc.. Fortunately, all those affects can be regarded as noise sources in our analysis. Thus the problem turned out to be: how to consider those noise sources in the integration, or in other words, how to get a real picture from the one which taken by a bad camera (bad lens or not well focused). Such a problem can be solved by using computer picture processing or imaging techniques.

In conclusion, we have calculated the potential and the magnetic field produced by a trapped fluxon in superconducting thin films based on monopole model. We have shown, to solve this kind SQUID imaging problem, it is better to divide into two steps: (1) calculating the magnetic field distribution analytically based on monopole model (including higher terms in Eq.(3.15) for higher accuracy); (2) doing the modified integration by using computer picture processing techniques.

Acknowledgment
The authors thank Dr. J. Yuyama for his useful discussion and Mr. K. Chihara for his assistant on computer graphics.

Reference
1. B. Cabrera, Ph.D. Thesis, Stanford University, (1975).

2. Junpei Yuyama, Masahiko Kasuya, Shun-ichi Kobayashi, L. Boesten, and Eiichi Goto, Proceedings of the 5th RIKEN symposium on Josephson Electronics, 110(1988).

3. A. Barone, and G. Paterno, Physics and Applications of the Josephson Effect, John Willy & Sons, Inc. (1982).

4. Yutaka Harada, Hideaki Nakane, Nobuo Miyamoto, Ushio Kawabe, Eiichi Goto, and Takashi Soma, IEEE Trans. on Magnetics, Mag-23, 3801(1987).

5. Tsuyoshi Matsuda, Shuji Hasegawa, Masukazu Igarashi, Toshio Kobayashi, Masayoshi Naito, Hiroshi Kajiyama, Junji Endo, Nobuyuki Osakabe, and Akira Tonomura, Phys. Rev. Lett. 62, 2519(1989).

Appendix
Green Function Solution for Trapped Fluxon on Large Superconducting Thin Film.

If we neglect the superconducting current which generated within the penetration depth, we can simplify the problem as:

a) A thin superconducting film is placed on z=0 plane with a normal hole of radius a. Since a ($\approx$ 0.05 µm) is much smaller than both the dimension of the superconducting film ($\geq$ 5 mm) and the distance between pick-up coil and film ($\approx$ 20 µm), the plate can be regarded as infinite one;

b) On upper half space, we have

$$\nabla \times \vec{B} = 0 . \tag{A.1}$$

Since

$$\vec{B} = \nabla \Phi \tag{A.2}$$

thus we obtain

$$\nabla^2 \Phi = 0 . \tag{A.3}$$

c) The boundary conditions are:

$$B_z\big|_{z=0} = \begin{cases} 0 & \text{if } R' \geq a \\ B_0 = \dfrac{\Phi_0}{\pi a^2} & \text{if } R' < a \end{cases} \tag{A.4}$$

The Green function for such boundary conditions in cylindrical coordinate is:

$$G(\vec{x}, \vec{x'}) = C' \left[\left[R^2 + z^2 + R'^2 + z'^2 - 2zz' - 2RR'\cos(\phi - \phi') \right]^{-1/2} \right.$$
$$\left. + \left[R^2 + z^2 + R'^2 + z'^2 + 2zz' - 2RR'\cos(\phi - \phi') \right]^{-1/2} \right] \tag{A.5}$$

By using the Green Formula

$$\int_{V'} (G\nabla^2\Phi - \Phi\nabla^2 G) \, dV' = \int_S [G\frac{\partial \Phi}{\partial n} - \Phi\frac{\partial G}{\partial n}] \, dS \tag{A.6}$$

we obtain the magnetic potential in upper space

$$\Phi(\vec{x}) = \int_S G(\vec{x},\vec{x'}) \frac{\partial \Phi(\vec{x'})}{\partial n} \, dS$$

$$= C' \int_0^a R'dR' \int_0^{2\pi} \left[R^2+z^2+R'^2-2zz'-2RR'\cos(\phi-\phi')\right]^{-1/2} d\phi'$$

$$(A.7)$$

since

$$\nabla^2 G = -\delta(\vec{x}-\vec{x'}) \tag{A.8}$$

$$\frac{\partial G}{\partial n} = 0. \tag{A.9}$$

For a place where $R^2+z^2 \gg a^2$, we use Taylor expansion and obtain the magnetic potential

$$\Phi(\vec{x}) = \frac{\pi a^2 C'}{(R^2+z^2)^{1/2}}\left[1 - \frac{a^2}{4(R^2+z^2)} + \frac{3a^2R^2}{8(R^2+z^2)^2}\right]. \tag{A.10}$$

The magnetic field therefore is

$$B_z = -\frac{\partial \Phi}{\partial z} = \frac{\pi a^2 C'z}{(R^2+z^2)^{1/2}}\left[1 - \frac{3a^2}{4(R^2+z^2)} + \frac{15a^2R^2}{8(R^2+z^2)^2}\right] \tag{A.11}$$

where the constant C' is determined by normalization equation

$$\Phi_0 = 2\pi \int_0^\infty RB_z \, dR = 2\pi^2 a^2 C'. \tag{A.12}$$

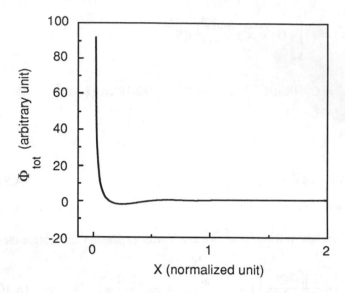

Figure 1. Magnetic potential, arised from a point charge in the center of superconducting circle, as a function of X at z = 0 plane.

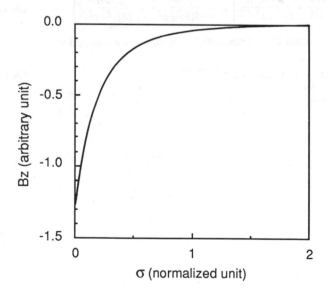

Figure 2. Magnetic field distribution as a function of $\sigma = \sqrt{X^2 - 1}$ at z = 0 plane.

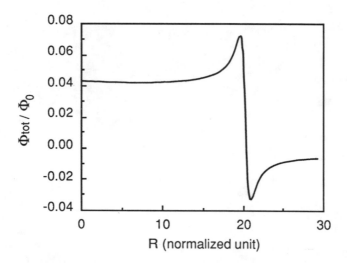

Figure 3. The flux passed through an one-loop coil as a function of the distance between the center axes of the coil and the superconducting circle.

Three Dimensional Inductance Calculation
- Methodology and CAD for Superconducting Coils and Transformers

Mutsumi Hosoya

Abstract

An effective method of calculating three dimensional inductance is derived. The methodology is extended to an analysis & design system for superconducting circuits. Several kinds of superconducting circuits are analyzed using this system.

Acknowledgements

I would like to express my sincere gratitude to Professor Goto for suggestions, advice, and continuous encouragement. I would also like to express my thanks to Messers. T. Soma, Y. Harada, N. Shimizu, N. Miyamoto for their variable discussions and suggestions. I also wish to thank Miss. Iwasaki for her technical assistance.

Most of this research has been supported by the Research Development Corporation of Japan. Numerical calculations have been done using the very large (super) computers of Hitachi Central Research Laboratory and the Institute of Physical and Chemical Research.

I. Introduction

Because Josephson devices have so much more potentiality than conventional silicon devices, great efforts are being made to use them for digital and analog applications. This chapter summarizes the basis of Josephson devices. First, the background of Josephson devices is outlined. Then, it discusses Josephson junctions and superconducting inductors, which are two major components of Josephson devices. Last, the scope of this paper is shown.

I-I. Josephson Device

Perfect conductivity, which is one of the most distinctive feature of superconductivity, was discovered by Onnes in 1911.[1] Subsequently, other characteristics were found, such as Meissner effect,[2] the existence of critical temperature (T_c) and critical magnetic field (H_c).

Efforts have since been made to interpret these phenomena. The first successful results were London's equations derived by F. London and H. London.[3] These equations could explain perfect conductivity and Meissner effect. Then, Ginzburg and Landau produced the Ginzburg-Landau equations,[4] in which quantum-mechanical characteristics of superconductors are partially considered. Last, in 1957, the complete quantum-mechanical explanation was given by Bardeen, Cooper and Schrieffer.[5] This reinforced previous theories. Based on the BCS theory, Josephson predicted in 1962 the effects of superconducting tunnel current in weakly coupled superconducting regions (Josephson junctions). These effects were experimentally confirmed by Anderson and Rowell in 1963.

Josephson devices use these Josephson junctions as active elements and superconducting inductors as passive elements as well as wiring for connections. Josephson devices have great advantages over conventional silicon devices as follows:

(1) Very fast switching speed of Josephson junctions $(O\,(psec))$

(2) Very low power dissipation $(O\,(nW))$ (Fig. 1-1)

(3) Strong non-linearity of Josephson junctions

(4) Low thermal noise

(5) Almost zero-loss/distortion wiring even at high frequency operation.

Because of these attractive features of Josephson devices, great efforts are being made in both digital and analog applications.[6, 7, 8, 9]

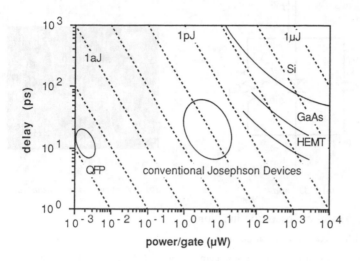

Fig. 1-1. Power-delay characteristics of Josephson devices

I-II. Josephson Junction

As stated above, Josephson devices are composed of Josephson junctions and superconducting inductors. Therefore, for the development of a Josephson device system it is very important to investigate these two components.

The operations of Josephson junctions are described by Josephson equations. It is known that Josephson junctions are well approximated by the RSJ model when Josephson penetration depth λ_J is greater than the size of the Josephson junctions (Fig. 1-2).[10]

The RSJ model comprises a tunneling current $I_m\sin\phi$, a non-linear conductance G_J, and a capacitance C_J. ϕ is the difference in phase of the Josephson junction as determined by the Josephson equations. I_m, G_J and C_J are determined by the shape and materials of the Josephson junction. Usually the shape and the materials of Josephson junctions are constant for the application.

Hence, the operations of Josephson junctions can be well simulated by the RSJ model if these parameters are obtained from a previous experiment.

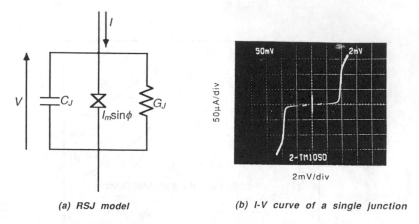

(a) RSJ model   (b) I-V curve of a single junction

Fig. 1-2. Model of Josephson junction

(a) is an RSJ model of a Josephson junction.

(b) is an I-V curve of a niobium-nitride/niobium oxide/lead-alloy junction, which gives non linear admittance of a Josephson junction.

On the other hand, the most distinctive value characterizing the operation of a superconducting inductor is inductance. It is calculated from the energy of a magnetic field induced by current. Superconducting inductors are discussed in the following.

I-III. Superconducting Inductor

The operations of superconducting inductors are determined by London's equations ((1-1)-(1-2)) and Maxwell's equations ((1-3)-(1-4)),

$$\nabla \times J_s = -\frac{1}{\lambda_L^2} H \tag{1-1}$$

$$\frac{\partial J_s}{\partial t} = \frac{1}{\mu_0 \lambda_L^2} E \tag{1-2}$$

$$\nabla \times H = J + \frac{\partial D}{\partial t} \tag{1-3}$$

$$\nabla \times E = -\frac{\partial B}{\partial t}, \tag{1-4}$$

where J_s is superconducting current density, J is total current density, λ_L is London penetration depth, H is magnetic field, B is magnetic flux density, E is electric field and D is dielectric flux density.

London's equations describe the superconducting current distribution inside a superconductor, when the gradient of the superconducting current density is small.

When the current distribution is static, no electric field exists due to (1-2). Hence, only superconducting current described by (1-1) flows. Combining (1-1) and (1-3),

$$\nabla \cdot \nabla H - \frac{1}{\lambda_L^2} H = 0 \tag{1-5}$$

is obtained. (1-5) can be solved if the boundary condition is given, and J_s is obtained from (1-1) and H.

When the current distribution changes, an electric field is induced by (1-2), and normal current flows. Let's consider the simple example shown in Fig. 1-3.

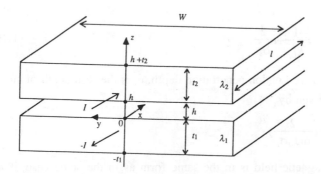

Fig. 1-3. Stripline model when the fringe effect can be neglected.

When $l \gg W \gg h$, the fringe effect can be neglected. In that case, only E_x and H_y are non-zero. When the current changes by the angular frequency ω, $\dfrac{E_x}{i\omega\mu_0\lambda_{L_i}^2}$

supercurrent flows according to (1-2). Therefore, the ratio of normal current to super current is given by

$$r=\left|\frac{\sigma_i E_x}{\dfrac{E_x}{i\omega\mu_0\lambda_{L_i}^2}}\right|=\omega\mu_0\lambda_{L_i}^2\sigma_i \qquad (1\text{-}6)$$

where σ_i is the normal conductivity of superconductor i. If $\omega=2\pi\times10^{10}$(10 G Hz operation), $r<0.2$ at around 4.2 K for a niobium thin film. This means that almost all current is super-current as determined by (1-1) even at 10 G Hz operation. Moreover, because displacement current is small in this case, (1-3) and (1-4) can be rewritten as

$$-\frac{\partial H_y}{\partial z}=\frac{E_x}{i\omega\mu_0\lambda_{L_i}^2}+\sigma_i E_x, \qquad (1\text{-}7)$$

$$\frac{\partial E_x}{\partial z}=-i\omega\mu_0 H_y \qquad (1\text{-}8)$$

From (1-7) and (1-8),

$$\frac{\partial^2 H_y}{\partial z^2}-\frac{1}{\lambda_i^2}H_y=0, \qquad (1\text{-}9)$$

where

$$\frac{1}{\lambda_i^2}=\frac{1}{\lambda_{L_i}^2}+i\frac{2}{\delta_i^2}. \qquad (1\text{-}10)$$

λ_i is the effective London penetration depth, δ_i is the skin depth of superconductor i and is given by

$$\delta_i=(\frac{2}{\omega\mu_0\sigma_i})^{1/2}. \qquad (1\text{-}11)$$

Thus, the magnetic field is in the same form as in the static case, if λ_i is used instead of λ_{L_i}. Because $\delta_i \gg \lambda_{L_i}$ for 10 G Hz operation, $\lambda_i \approx \lambda_{L_i}$. Therefore, even at 10 G Hz operation, H and J_s do not change as much as in the static case. (I'll discuss a more rigorous treatment for superconducting striplines later.)

I-IV. Scope of Study in This Paper

As shown above, the inductance of a superconducting inductor can be calculated by (1-1) and (1-3) under specified boundary conditions. However, when the boundary condition becomes three-dimensional, it is very difficult to solve this problem using restricted computational resources. Chapter II discusses the methodology for solving this problem. This method is applicable not only to superconductors but also to inductors which operate at high frequency.

The major purpose of inductance calculations is the analysis and design of superconducting circuits. Therefore, the method described in Chapter II is extended to an analysis & design system for superconducting circuits. The system is discussed in Chapter III.

A superconducting stripline is the most elementary inductor. It is used not only for connections but also as a circuit element. In Chapter IV, the characteristics of superconducting striplines are discussed by analytical and numerical methods.

The SQUID circuit is one of the most practical superconducting circuits. The inductance plays a very important role in the operation of SQUID's.[11, 12] Chapter V discusses the inductance of a planar washer SQUID. The coupling characteristics of the SQUID is calculated for the three-dimensional model using the CAD system described in Chapter III.

A superconducting transformer is required for impedance matching or inverting logical signals of the QFP.[13, 14, 15, 16] Chapter VI describes superconducting transformers for the QFP circuits. Some kinds of transformers are analyzed using the CAD system.

II. Extrapolated Boundary Element Method

In the case of a nearly perfect conductor, i.e., when the skin depth δ (in ordinary conductors) or the London penetration depth δ_L (in superconductors) is much smaller than the other physical scales, the current flows only on the surface. Hence, the three-dimensional distribution of the magnetic field is fully specified by the two-dimensional current distribution (Boundary Elements) on the surface. The specific *BEM* (Boundary Element Method) is called *SCM* (Surface Current Method). In *SCM,* the surface is partitioned into N small areas, each with a looping current $I_i(1 \leq i \leq N)$. I_i's are determined by solving N simultaneous linear equations so as to eliminate the normal component of the magnetic field at the center of each area. The inductance is given in terms of the magnetic energy among N current loops. Thus, the problem is reduced to a two-dimensional one in *SCM*. To obtain the final results, the error estimate as a function of N is made and they are obtained as the extrapolation for N tending to infinity. Calculations for some examples including a fully three-dimensional object are presented. The effect of non-zero δ and δ_L can be, in the present *SCM,* made by thinning the object by the amount δ (if the width of the conductor is larger than δ) but the more rigorous treatment is discussed in III.

II-I. Introduction

The computation of inductance is very important for the design of circuitry and devices in Josephson junction technology, and various methods for inductance calculation are derived.[17, 18, 19] However, by these methods, when the current distribution is three-dimensional, the calculation becomes impossible because the requirements for the computation time or memory is too severe at current state.

In the case of a nearly perfect conductor, i.e., when the skin depth δ or the London penetration depth δ_L is much smaller than the other physical scales, the conductor is assumed to be perfect, and the current is assumed to flow only on the surface. Hence, the magnetic field of the system is fully specified by the two-dimensional current distribution on the surface.

If three-dimensional field problem is solved by computing the two-dimensional current distribution (Boundary Elements) on the surface, the requirements for computational resources are much reduced, which enables the calculation of an object with more complex shape. In this chapter, a new variant of *BEM*, called *Surface Current Method (SCM)* which follows the above scheme, is introduced. Calculations for some examples including a fully three-dimensional object are presented. The error of *SCM* is discussed in relation to the influence of the extrapolation, which is used in order to obtain the final result effectively.

II-II. Principles of SCM

In *SCM*, the surface is partitioned into N small areas, each with a looping current I_i $(1 \leq i \leq N)$. Let the normal component of the magnetic field at the center of looping current I_i be H_i. Then, H_i can be written as the linear combination of I_i as shown in (2-1).

$$H_i = \sum_{j=0}^{N} a_{ij} I_j, \tag{2-1}$$

where a_{ij} is a constant determined by the shape of the conductor and can be calculated directly from the positions of I_i and I_j. I_0 is any current path flowing the whole conductor. Because the current is re-distributed by the condition described below, there is no restriction on the path where I_0 flows even if it is chosen to flow the whole conductor.

H_i must be 0 because the conductor is perfect. Hence, I_i can be obtained by solving the simultaneous linear equations (2-2).

$$
\begin{bmatrix}
1 & 0 & . & 0 \\
a_{10} & . & . & . \\
. & a_{ij} & . & . \\
. & . & . & a_{NN}
\end{bmatrix}
\begin{bmatrix}
I_0 \\
I_1 \\
. \\
I_N
\end{bmatrix}
=
\begin{bmatrix}
I \\
0 \\
. \\
0
\end{bmatrix}
\tag{2-2}
$$

where I is the current of the source.

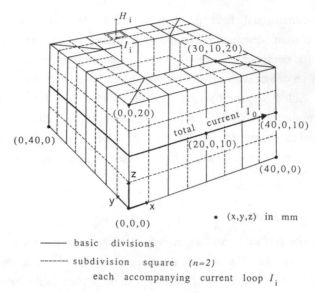

Fig. 2-1 Divisions of the surface of a square block

Divisions of the surface of a square block are illustrated. I_0 flows on the outer surface in this figure. Coordinates of fig. 2-1 correspond to those of fig. 2-2.

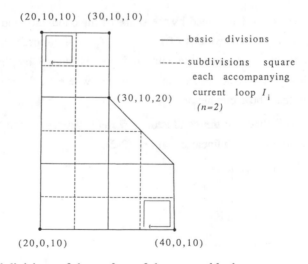

Fig. 2-2 Subdivisions of the surface of the square block

Subdivisions of the surface of the square block are illustrated. Each subdivision has a current loop.

The inductance L is given in terms of the magnetic field energy among current loops as shown in (2-3).

$$L=\frac{1}{I^2}\sum_{i,j}M_{ij}I_iI_j,\qquad\qquad(2\text{-}3)$$

where M_{ij} is the mutual inductance between current loops i and j, and can be calculated directly from the positions of the current loops as shown in II-III.

Therefore, the inductance of a three-dimensional object is reduced to a two dimensional one in *SCM*, which may be regarded as a special case of *BEM*.

II-III. Mutual inductance integral

Mutual inductance integral between two lines: $P_1(x_1,y_1,z_1)\rightarrow P_2(x_2,y_2,z_2)$ and $P_3(x_3,y_3,z_3)\rightarrow P_4(x_4,y_4,z_4)$ is given by

$$M=\int_0^{r_{12}}du\int_0^{r_{34}}dv\frac{c}{r(u,v)},\qquad\qquad(2\text{-}4)$$

where c is the cosine of the angle between $\overrightarrow{P_1P_2}$ and $\overrightarrow{P_3P_4}$, $r(u,v)$ is the distance between $P_1+\overrightarrow{P_2P_1}\dfrac{u}{r_{12}}$ and $P_3+\overrightarrow{P_4P_3}\dfrac{v}{r_{34}}$, and r_{ij} is the distance between P_i and P_j. Hence,

$$c=\frac{(P_1-P_2)(P_3-P_4)}{r_{12}r_{34}}\qquad\qquad(2\text{-}5)$$

$$r(u,v)=\left[u^2+v^2+r_{13}^2-2cuv-2b_1u-2b_2v\right]^{1/2},\qquad\qquad(2\text{-}6)$$

where

$$b_1=\frac{(P_2-P_1)(P_3-P_1)}{r_{12}}\qquad\qquad(2\text{-}7)$$

$$b_2=\frac{(P_4-P_3)(P_1-P_3)}{r_{34}}\qquad\qquad(2\text{-}8)$$

Let d be the minimum distance between the above two lines extended to infinity. In the following, the evaluation of M is classified according to the value of c and d.

II-III-I. In the non parallel case, $|c| \neq 1$

In this case,

$$d = r(u_0, v_0) \tag{2-9}$$

$$r(u,v) = r_0(u - u_0, v - v_0), \tag{2-10}$$

where

$$\begin{pmatrix} u_0 \\ v_0 \end{pmatrix} = \frac{1}{1-c^2} \begin{pmatrix} 1 & c \\ c & 1 \end{pmatrix} \begin{pmatrix} b_1 \\ b_2 \end{pmatrix} \tag{2-11}$$

$$r_0(x,y) = \left[x^2 + y^2 - 2cxy + d^2 \right]^{1/2} \tag{2-12}$$

Therefore,

$$M = \int_{-u_0}^{r_{12}-u_0} dx \int_{-v_0}^{r_{34}-v_0} dy \frac{c}{r_0(x,y)} \tag{2-13}$$

The above integral is given by the following indefinite integral:

$$\int dx \int dy \frac{c}{r_0(x,y)} = g(x,y) + h(x,y), \tag{2-14}$$

where

$$g(x,y) = \int dx \int dy \left[\frac{c}{r_0(x,y)} + \frac{cd^2}{r_0(x,y)^3} \right]$$

$$= y\log(x - cy + r_0(x,y)) + x\log(y - cx + r_0(x,y)) \tag{2-15}$$

$$h(x,y) = \int dx \int dy \frac{-cd^2}{r_0(x,y)^3}$$

$$= \frac{cd}{s} \arctan \frac{s r_0(x,y) d}{xys^2 + cd^2} \tag{2-16}$$

$$=\frac{cd}{s}\text{ATAN2}(sr_0(x,y)d,xys^2+cd^2) \qquad (2\text{-}16)'$$

$$s=(1-c^2)^{1/2} \qquad (2\text{-}17)$$

In numerical calculation, the FORTRAN function ATAN2 should be used for proper branch selection of the arctan function. Hence,

$$M=g\,(r_{12}-u_0,r_{34}-v_0)+g\,(-u_0,-v_0)$$

$$-g\,(r_{12}-u_0,-v_0)-g\,(-u_0,r_{34}-v_0)$$

$$+h\,(r_{12}-u_0,r_{34}-v_0)+h\,(-u_0,-v_0)$$

$$-h\,(r_{12}-u_0,-v_0)-h\,(-u_0,r_{34}-v_0) \qquad (2\text{-}18)$$

II-III-II. In the (anti) parallel case, $|c|=1$

From Fig. 2-3 and the definitions of b_1 and b_2, we see the identity:

$$b_2=-cb_1 \qquad (2\text{-}19)$$

$$r(u,v)=\left[(u-c(v-b_2))^2+d^2\right]^{1/2} \qquad (2\text{-}20)$$

$$d^2=r_{13}^2-b_1^2 \qquad (2\text{-}21)$$

Hence,

$$M=\int\limits_0^{r_{12}} du \int\limits_{b_1}^{cr_{34}+b_1} dw\,\frac{1}{r_p(u,w)}, \qquad (2\text{-}22)$$

where

$$w=c(v-b_2) \qquad (2\text{-}23)$$

$$r_p(u,w)=\left[(u-w)^2+d^2\right]^{1/2} \qquad (2\text{-}24)$$

56

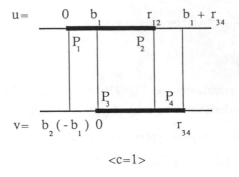

$u= \quad 0 \quad b_1 \qquad\qquad r_{12} \quad b_1 + r_{34}$

$v= \quad b_2(-b_1)\ 0 \qquad\qquad r_{34}$

<c=1>

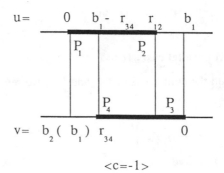

$u= \quad 0 \quad b_1 - r_{34} \quad r_{12} \quad b_1$

$v= \quad b_2(\ b_1\ )\ r_{34} \qquad\qquad 0$

<c=-1>

Fig. 2-3 Diagrams for two parallel current segments

Diagrams for two current segments when $d{\neq}0$ are shown.

II-III-II-I. When $d{\neq}0$

The above definite integral is given by the following indefinite integral:

$$\int dx \int dy \frac{1}{r_p(x,y)} = g_p(x,y)+r_p(x,y), \qquad (2\text{-}25)$$

where

$$g_p(x,y)=y\log(x{-}y{+}r_p(x,y))+x\log(y{-}x{+}r_p(x,y)) \qquad (2\text{-}26)$$

Therefore,

$$M=g_p(r_{12},c(r_{34}{-}b_2))+g_p(0,{-}cb_2)$$

$$-g_p(r_{12},-cb_2)-g_p(0,c(r_{34}-b_2))$$

$$+r_{24}+r_{13}-r_{23}-r_{14} \qquad (2\text{-}27)$$

II-III-II-II. When $d=0$

$$M=\int_0^{r_{12}} du \int_{b_1}^{cr_{34}+b_1} dw < \frac{1}{|w-u|}$$

$$= |b_1-r_{12}|\log|b_1-r_{12}|+|cr_{34}+b_1|\log|cr_{34}+b_1|$$

$$-|b_1|\log|b_1|-|cr_{34}+b_1-r_{12}|\log|cr_{34}+b_1-r_{12}| \qquad (2\text{-}28)$$

II-IV. Extrapolation error of SCM

In *SCM,* the surface is divided into N_0 basic divisions at first. Then, each basic division is subdivided into n subdivisions for each dimension. That is, total number of subdivisions, N, is $N_0 n^2$ for a three-dimensional object. The calculation is performed for various n's and the results are extrapolated to obtain the final inductance. The reason why the surface is divided in two steps (basic and sub) is for increasing the effectiveness of the extrapolation. In FEM (Finite Element Method), the element division is executed mainly by experience. By this method, the shape of elements has irregularity, which decreases the effectiveness of extrapolations. In *SCM,* because such irregularity is absorbed by the basic divisions and the extrapolation is performed on the regular subdivisions, it is expected to work more effectively.

The extrapolation enables the effective anticipation of the true inductance, i.e., the value at $n=\infty$. If the inductance can be computed from relatively small n's, much time and memory for the calculation can be reduced.

In the following, the extrapolation and the error of extrapolation are considered.

II-IV-I. Extrapolation and Error polynomial

If the number of subdivision n is an integer, we can only use the following n sampling points to obtain an unknown value,

$$f(n), f(n-1), f(n-2), \cdots, f(1).$$

Let $x = \dfrac{1}{n}$. We must anticipate the extrapolated value at $x=0 (n=\infty)$ effectively. If the original function is a polynomial of degree k in x, the exact value can be obtained from the following $k+1$ points,

$$f(n), f(n-1), f(n-2), \cdots, f(n-k).$$

We use the polynomial defined from the above $k+1$ points as an extrapolation polynomial $P_{n,k}$. Hence,

$$P_{n,k}(\lambda_i f(n-i);x)$$

$$= \frac{1}{k!} \sum_{i=0}^{k} (-1)^i \binom{k}{i} (n-i)^k f(n-i) \prod_{\substack{j=0 \\ j\neq i}}^{k} \left[1-(n-j)x \right]. \qquad (2\text{-}29)$$

The error polynomial is defined as follows:

$$Z_{n,k}(\lambda_i f(n-i)) \equiv P_{n,k}(\lambda_i f(n-i);0) \qquad (2\text{-}30\text{-}1)$$

$$= \frac{1}{k!} \sum_{i=0}^{k} (-1)^i \binom{k}{i} (n-i)^k f(n-i) \qquad (2\text{-}30\text{-}2)$$

$$= \frac{1}{k!} \Delta_n{}^k (n^k f(n)), \qquad (2\text{-}30\text{-}3)$$

where

$$\Delta_n f(n) = f(n) - f(n-1) \qquad (2\text{-}31\text{-}1)$$

$$\Delta_n{}^{k+1} f(n) = \Delta_n{}^k \cdot \Delta_n f(n). \qquad (2\text{-}31\text{-}2)$$

If f is decomposed into two parts as

$$f(n) = \sum_{i=0}^{k} a_i n^{-i} + g(n)$$

then

$$Z_{n,k}(\lambda_i f(n-i)) = \frac{1}{k!} \Delta_n{}^k (n^k f(n)) \qquad (2\text{-}32\text{-}1)$$

$$=\frac{1}{k!}\sum_{i=0}^{k}a_i\Delta_n{}^k(n^{k-i})+\frac{1}{k!}\Delta_n{}^k(n^k g(n)) \qquad (2\text{-}32\text{-}2)$$

$$=a_0+Z_{n,k}(\lambda_i g(n-i)) \qquad (2\text{-}32\text{-}3)$$

because

$$\Delta_n{}^k(n^{k-m})=0 \qquad (1\leq m\leq k). \qquad (2\text{-}33)$$

Hence, $Z_{n,k}(\lambda_i g(n-i))$ is the error from $a_0=f(\infty)$. In table 2-1, the results of the calculation $Z_{n,k}(\lambda_i g(n-i))$ are summarized for the various forms of g. We can analyze the error by changing k, n and examining which type the original function may be.

II-IV-II. Round off error

If each f_i contains an error by ε,

$$|Z_{n,k}|\leq\frac{\varepsilon}{k!}\sum_{i=0}^{k}\binom{k}{i}(n-i)^k \qquad (2\text{-}34)$$

Therefore, maximum of k, k_{max} is determined by (2-35).

$$\max|Z_{n,k}|<\delta \qquad (2\text{-}35)$$

ε is caused by the round off error, and varies according to the precision of a number. δ is the maximum (absolute) error to be permitted. In table 2-2, k_{max} is calculated for some cases. As shown in table 2-2, k must not be so large.

Table 2-1. $Z_{n,k}$ for various $g(n)$'s

$g(n)$	$Z_{n,k}$ $(n \gg k)$
$\dfrac{1}{n^{k+j}}$	$_{k+j-1}C_k \dfrac{(-1)^k}{n^{k+j}}$
$\dfrac{1}{n^j}\log n$	$\dfrac{(-1)^{j-1}}{_kC_j j n^j}$
$n^{-\frac{1}{j}}$	$(\dfrac{e}{kn})^{\frac{1}{j}}\ (k \gg 1)$

Table 2-2. k_{max} determined by the round off error

n	$\varepsilon=16^{-6}$			$\varepsilon=16^{-14}$			
	$\delta=10^{-2}$	$\delta=10^{-3}$	$\delta=10^{-4}$	$\delta=10^{-2}$	$\delta=10^{-4}$	$\delta=10^{-6}$	$\delta=10^{-8}$
8	8	8	4	8	8	8	8
12	7	4	3	12	12	12	12
16	5	3	2	16	16	16	16
20	3	3	2	20	20	20	11
24	4	3	2	24	24	13	9
28	3	2	2	20	16	11	7
32	2	2	1	18	13	10	7

II-IV-III. Singularity of $g(n)$

If g(n) has a singular point at n_0 such as

$$g(n) = \frac{1}{n - n_0} \qquad (2\text{-}36)$$

then,

$$|Z_{n,k}(\lambda_i g(n-i))| = \frac{1}{k!} \Delta_n{}^k \left(\frac{n^k}{n - n_0} \right) \qquad (2\text{-}37)$$

If k becomes too close to n, the value of (2-37) increases. When $n_0 = 1$, k_{opt} which optimize (2-37) is shown in table 2-3. This is the second reason that k should no be so large.

Table 2-3. k_{opt} when $g(n)$ has a pole

n	k_{opt}
8	6
12	4
16	3
20	3
24	2
28	2
32	2

II-V. Some examples

Based on the analysis considered in the previous section, the error analyses are performed on some examples. The results are compared to the experimental data or a theoretical value. The results of these error analyses indicate the accuracy of the calculation by *SCM*.

62

II-V-I. Annulus

First example is the inductance of the thin annulus shown in Fig. 2-4.

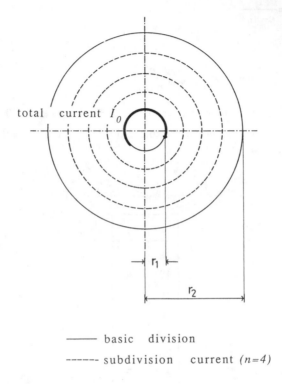

——— basic division

------ subdivision current *(n=4)*

Fig. 2-4 Thin annulus

If r_2 is infinite, the inductance can be calculated analytically.

If r_2 is infinite, the inductance is given by (2-38).

$$L=2r_1\mu, \qquad\qquad (2\text{-}38)$$

where μ is the permeability of the conductor. The annulus is subdivided into n small areas in radial direction. Because of the rotational symmetry, the problem is reduced to a one-dimensional one. Mutual inductance between two current segment loops is given by (2-39) and (2-40).

$$M_{ij}=2\mu\frac{(R_iR_j)^{1/2}}{k}\left\{(1-\frac{k^2}{2})K(k)-E(k)\right\} \qquad\qquad (2\text{-}39)$$

$$k^2 = \frac{4R_i R_j}{(R_i + R_j)^2}, \tag{2-40}$$

where R_i, R_j is the radius of each loop and $K(k), E(k)$ are complete elliptic integrals of the first and second kind. The inductance calculation is done for various r_2's and n's. The results are extrapolated in both directions and compared to (2-38). They are summarized in Fig. 2-5 and 2-6, where $r_1 = 1$ and the extrapolation for r_2 is performed by the quadratic polynomial determined by 3 points at $r_2 = 1, 2, 4$.

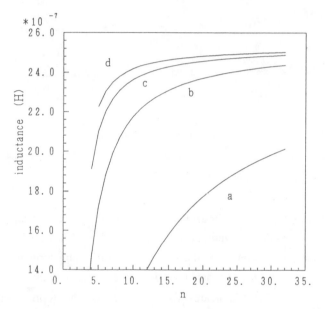

Fig. 2-5 Inductance of the thin annulus

Inductance of the thin annulus is calculated and extrapolated for r_2 and n. As for r_2 direction, values are extrapolated by the quadratic polynomial. As for n direction, the results are extrapolated by the polynomials of $\frac{1}{n}$. a is the values without extrapolation. b, c, and d are the values extrapolated by the polynomials of $-1, -2$, and -3 degree in n respectively.

64

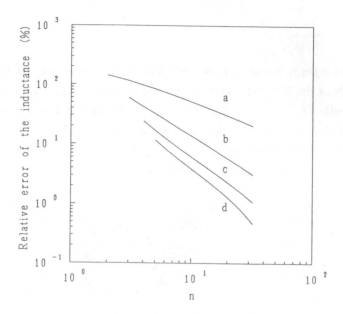

Fig. 2-6 Relative error of the inductance of the thin annulus

Results of fig. 2-5 are compared to the analytical value, and the errors are plotted. Curve numbers correspond to those of fig. 2-5.

As shown in Fig. 2-6, the inductance is obtained with 1 % relative error at $n \geq 19$ by the extrapoltion polynomial of degree -3 in n. The slope of a line in Fig 2-6 indicates the exponent of the primarily contributing term in $Z_{n,k}$. The slope is smaller than $-(i+1)$ when the highest exponent of the extrapolating function is $-i$. This fact indicates the existence of the term with smaller exponent in the extrapolating function.

II-V-II. Parallel thin plates

Second example is the inductance of an infinitely long, parallel thin plates shown in Fig 2-7. Current of two plates are the same and the direction is reversed.

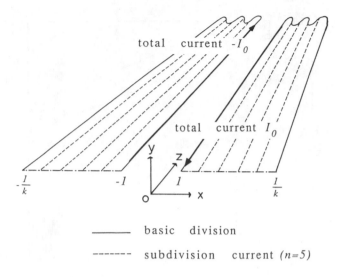

basic   division

------- subdivision   current *(n=5)*

Fig. 2-7 Parallel thin plates

Inductance of this system can be obtained analytically. In *SCM*, calculations are performed for current segments with finite spacing to avoid the divergence of the mutual inductance between segments.

The inductance is given by (2-41).

$$L = \mu \frac{K(k)}{K'(k)}, \tag{2-41}$$

where $K'(k)$ is the complementary function of $K(k)$. In order to avoid the divergence of the inductance, calculations are performed for the current segments with finite spacing. The influence of this finite spacing is $O(\frac{1}{n}\log n)$ and can be eliminated by the extrapolation. In Fig. 2-8, convergence for various extrapolating functions are plotted.

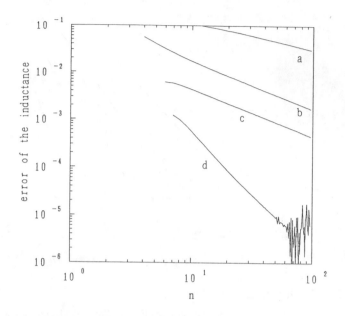

Fig. 2-8 Inductance of the parallel thin plates

The results of the calculation are extrapolated by various functions. a is the value without extrapolation (L). b is $\Delta_n(n\Delta_n(nL))$ by which $\dfrac{1}{n},\dfrac{1}{n}\log n$ terms are eliminated. c is $\dfrac{1}{4}\Delta_n^2(n^2\Delta_n^2(n^2L))$ by which $\dfrac{1}{n^2},\dfrac{1}{n},\dfrac{1}{n^2}\log n,\dfrac{1}{n}\log n$ terms are eliminated. In d, $\dfrac{1}{n^2},\dfrac{1}{n},\dfrac{1}{n^2}\log n,\dfrac{1}{n}\log n,\dfrac{1}{n}(\log n)^2$ terms are eliminated.

II-V-III. Square block with a square hole

Last example is the inductance of a square block with a square hole shown in Fig. 2-1. (Sub)divisions of the object is also shown in Fig. 2-1 and 2-2. Mutual inductance between two current segments is calculated by the equations described in II-III. Current distribution on the surface is plotted in Fig. 2-9.

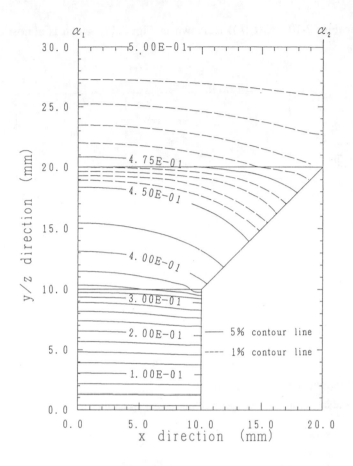

Fig. 2-9 Current distribution of the square block

Current distribution of the square block of fig. 2-1 is shown. Almost all current flows inner surface.

At line α_1, 66 percents of the whole current flows on the inner surface, 28 percents on the upper(lower) surface, and the rest on the outer surface. At line α_2, 76 percents of the whole current flows on the inner surface, 21 percents on the upper(lower) surface, and the rest on the outer surface. Therefore, 10 percents flows into the inner surface from the upper(lower) surface between line α_1 and α_2. The current density increases near the corner. The inductance $L(n)$ is plotted in Fig. 2-10. $\Delta_n(L(n))$ is shown in Fig. 2-11, which is almost equal to $dL(n)/dn$.

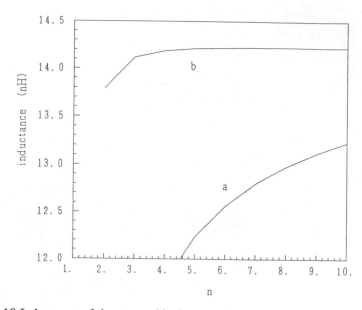

Fig. 2-10 Inductance of the square block

Inductance of the square block is calculated (a) and extrapolated by the polynomial of -1 degree in n (b).

Fig. 2-11 indicates that the primarily contributing term of $L(n)$ is n^{-1}. Therefore, $L(n)$ is extrapolated by the polynomial of degree -1 in n. The extrapolated value $a_0 + \Delta_n(nL(n))$ and its differential value $\Delta_n^2(nL(n))$ are plotted also in Fig. 2-10 and 2-11. As shown in Fig. 2-11, $\Delta_n^2(nL(n)) \approx 50n^{-5}$. Therefore, $\Delta_n(nL(n)) \approx 10n^{-4}$ and the extrapolation error is about 10^{-3} at $n=10$ which corresponds to less than 0.01 % relative error.

69

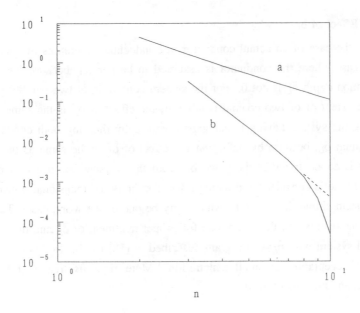

Fig. 2-11 Error of the inductance of the square block

Because $\Delta_n(L)\approx O(n^{-2})$, L is extrapolated by the polynomial of -1 degree in n. Differential of the error polynomial, $\Delta_n^2(nL)\approx O(n^{-5})$.

The inductance measurement is actually performed on the model in the condition that the current frequency is 32 M Hz.[20] In the case, δ is 11.6 μ m and the conductor is assumed to be perfect. The measured inductance is 14.2 n H which agrees with the calculation completely.

The computational complexity of the computation is $O(n^4)$ to calculate H_i, $O(n^4)$ to calculate M_{ij}, and $O(n^6)$ to solve the simultaneous linear equation. However, because actual n's are small and because it is unnecessary to calculate M_{ij} when two current segments are vertical, the most costing calculation is H_i. When $n=10$ and $N=455$, CPU time to obtain the current distribution (set the matrix elements and solve it) is about 15 minutes and to compute the inductance is about 10 minutes by Fujitsu M380.

II-VI. Effect of δ_L

In the case of an actual conductor, the inductance increases in comparison to the case where the conductor is assumed to be perfect, because the London penetration depth δ_L is not 0. For the system consisting of two parallel plane of infinite extent or of two coaxial conductor, the effect of δ_L is the same as considering the system having larger gaps obtained by thinning both conductor by the amount δ_L, because by definition the effect of δ_L is the same as though the current is concentrated at the plane δ_L from the surface. As one of the rough estimation let's consider the thinning effect for the two dimensional transmission line system shown in Fig. 2-11 which may be one of the worst case. Table 2-4 shows the results of calculation, one for proper treatment of δ_L and the other for thinned system with δ_L=0 (program described in [18] used). In this case, agreement is acceptable for small penetration. More rigorous treatment for large penetration is discussed in III.

Table 2-4. Effect of δ_L

λ_L/t is the degree of penetration, L_{rig} is the inductance obtained by rigorous treatment and L_{app} is the inductance obtained by thinning approximation.

λ_L/t (%)	L_{rig} (p H / μ m)	L_{app} (p H / μ m)	error (%)
0	0.31740	0.31740	0
10	0.33917	0.34001	0.25
20	0.36203	0.36493	0.80
30	0.38718	0.39283	1.46
40	0.41542	0.42468	2.23
50	0.44782	0.46201	3.17
60	0.48516	0.50735	4.57
70	0.52790	0.56540	7.10
80	0.57640	0.64725	12.29
90	0.63085	0.78610	24.61

II-VII. Summary

In the case of a nearly perfect conductor, the current flows only on the surface. Hence, the magnetic field of the system is fully specified by the two-dimensional current distribution on the surface. In *SCM,* the surface is partitioned into N small areas, each with a looping current $I_i(1 \leq i \leq N)$. I_i's are determined by solving N simultaneous linear equations so as to eliminate the normal component of the magnetic field at the center of each area. The inductance is given in terms of the magnetic energy among N current loops. Therefore, the inductance of a three-dimensional object is reduced to a two-dimensional one in *SCM,* which enables the inductance calculation of an object with more complex shape.

In *SCM,* extrapolations are used to obtain the final result from small N's. By the extrapolation, the precision of the computation increases drastically. Moreover, the error estimate becomes possible by examining the extrapolation polynomial.

Reduction to a two dimensional problem and the use of extrapolations save much computational resources. When calculating the model shown in Fig. 2-12 with the accuracy of 0.06 % error, *SCM* only needs 0.3 % CPU time and 1.6 % Memory space required by the method described in[18] (Most of the saving seems to come from extrapolations.)

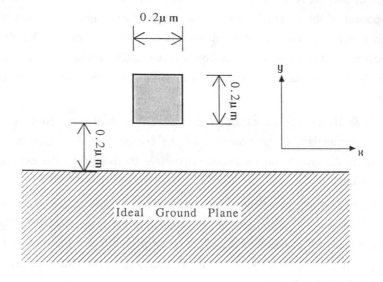

Fig. 2-12 Superconducting stripline

Effect of δ_L is estimated for the special case of superconducting stripline system. This system may be one of the worst case because if penetration is 100 % , the thinning approximation diverges.

Calculation for a fully three-dimensional object agrees well with experimental datum. More rigorous treatment of δ_L effect is discussed in III.

III. Inductance Calculation System for Superconducting Circuits

This chapter describes a method for calculating the inductance of complicated three-dimensional superconducting circuits. In this method, current distribution is obtained by solving the simultaneous linear equation which satisfies
both Maxwell's and London's equations. Inductance is calculated from magnetic energy caused by the current. Extrapolations are used to reduce the computational resources and to increase the accuracy of the results. Based upon the
method, a CAD system was developed to design superconducting circuits. The
inductance of complicated 3D superconducting circuits, which was unattainable
except by experiments, can be easily calculated by this system. Coupling inductance of a dc-SQUID is calculated using the CAD system. The result agrees
well with the experiment.

III-I. Introduction

The computation of inductance is very important for the design of circuitry
and devices in Josephson junction technology, and some calculation methods
have been reported in the case of two-dimensional problems.[18, 17] However,
three-dimensional analyses are often required in the design of real circuits which
are composed of complicated three-dimensional inductors.

The authors showed an effective method called *SCM* for calculating the
inductance of three-dimensional superconductors when London penetration
depth λ_L is much smaller than the other physical scales.[21] When the thickness
of a conductor is as thin as the London penetration depth, the influence of
current penetration should be treated rigorously. Therefore, a new method was
derived in which current distribution is determined by Maxwell's and London's
equations inside a conductor.

The discretization of current distribution is discussed in Sec. III-II and the
method of inductance calculation is explained in Sec. III-III. A CAD system for
the design of superconducting circuits is introduced in Sec. III-IV. An example
of a calculation by the CAD system is described in Sec. III-V.

74

III-II. Current Distribution

In this new method, a superconductor is divided into small blocks, and the centers of adjacent blocks are connected by edges. These edges produce a network (Fig. 3-1).

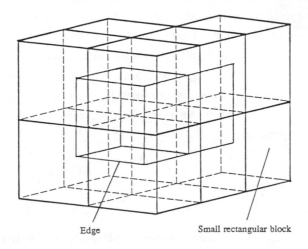

Edge   Small rectangular block

Fig. 3-1 Small rectangular blocks connected by edges

A superconductor is divided into small blocks, and the centers of adjacent blocks are connected by edges. These edges produce a network.

Current is assumed to flow only in these edges. Current distribution inside a conductor can be represented by the current flowing in this network.

In order to reduce memory resources, the number of variables should be as small as possible. If the number of edges and nodes are m and n respectively, the number of independent variables needed to specify the current distribution of the network uniquely is $m-n+1$ if all nodes of the network are connected.

It is possible to choose $m-n+1$ independent variables by calculating a fundamental current loop set, which can be adapted to general network systems. However, there exists a simpler method if the network has some restrictions. In the following, this simple method to choose the basis of cycles is discussed.

Simple network

Let $Y_i(i=1,2,\cdots,n)$ be a convex polygon, and E_i be the set of edges of Y_i. A convex polyhedron can be constructed by E_i, E_{i+1}, and $E_{i\,i+1}$, where $E_{i\,i+1}$ is a set of edges between vertexes of Y_i and Y_{i+1}.

The network composed of E_i $(i=1,2,\cdots,n)$ and $E_{i\,i+1}$ $(i=1,2,\cdots,n-1)$ produces a planar graph (Fig. 3-2).

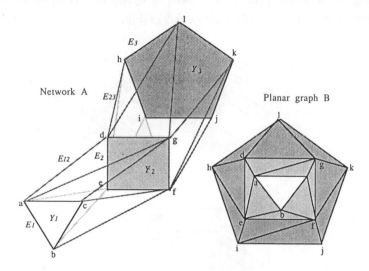

Fig. 3-2 Basis of cycles of simple network

A planar graph B can be constructed from a network A. Contours of all finite regions of B produce its basis of cycles. Therefore, the basis of cycles of A is given by contours of all planes except Y_2 and Y_3.

According to graph theory, the basis of cycles of a planar graph is given by contours of its finite regions. Therefore, the basis of cycles of the network is given by contours of all polyhedron planes except $Y_i(i=2,3,\cdots,n)$. We call this type of network a simple network.

Complex network

The following theorem can be proved:

Let G_{s1}, G_{s2} be planar connected graphs and L_{s1}, L_{s2} be the bases of the cycles of G_{s1}, G_{s2} respectively. Let G_1, G_2 be graphs and $L_1 \cup L_{s1}$, $L_2 \cup L_{s2}$ be the bases of the cycles of G_1, G_2 respectively. If G_{s1} and G_{s2} are identical as a graph, a new connected graph G can be constructed by replacing G_{s2} with G_{s1}. In this case, the base of cycles of G is $L_1 \cup L_2 \cup L_{s1}$.

Therefore, a complex network can be made by combining simple networks according to the above scheme. The basis of cycles of a complex network is given by the union of those of simple networks (Fig. 3-3).

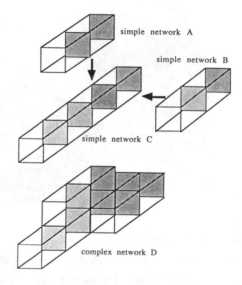

Fig. 3-3 Basis of cycles of complex network

The basis of cycles of each simple network is given by all boundaries of its transparent planes. The basis of cycles of complex network D is given by the union of those of simple networks.

Current path

If the circuit has a hole and current flows around a hole, flux is trapped in the hole. Current circulating around the hole is not 0 in this case. Hence, if there exists a hole in a circuit, the current path along the hole must be considered in addition to current cycles. Because the value of the current path is distributed by current cycles such that the current distribution satisfies physical laws, the current path may be any route around the hole.

Symmetry

If the current distribution is (anti-)symmetric against a plane, only half of the symmetric parts should be considered. If anti-symmetry exists against a plane, the directions of cycles of these two parts are opposite.

A symmetry plane may divide a cycle, and many symmetry planes may exist. Independent variables can be selected easily by considering simple networks and combining them. Fig. 3-4 explains the basis of cycles when three symmetry planes ($x=0$, $y=0$ and $z=0$) exist, and they divide cycles.

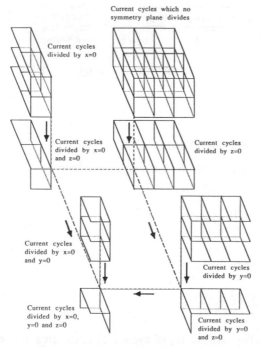

Fig. 3-4 Basis of current cycles with symmetry

Fig. 3-4 shows the basis of cycles when three symmetry planes ($x=0$, $y=0$ and $z=0$) exist, and they divide current cycles. Each plane above has a current cycle around its boundary. The basis is given by union of all these cycles.

III-III. Inductance Calculation

In this method, a superconducting circuit is approximated by small rectangular blocks. The centers of adjacent blocks are connected by edges. These edges construct a network. As discussed in Sec. III-II, current distribution of this network can be specified by cycles and paths as follows:

$$E = A \begin{bmatrix} L \\ P \end{bmatrix},$$

(3-1)

where E is value of edges, L is value of cycles, and P is value of paths.

If current E_{12} flows through edge $e_1 e_2$, magnetic field $\vec{H}$ caused by the current at o is given by:

$$\vec{H} = -\frac{E_{12}}{4\pi}\left(\frac{\overrightarrow{oe_1} \cdot \overrightarrow{e_1 e_2}}{|\overrightarrow{oe_1}|} + \frac{\overrightarrow{e_2 o} \cdot \overrightarrow{e_1 e_2}}{|\overrightarrow{e_2 o}|}\right)\frac{\overrightarrow{e_1 e_2} \times \overrightarrow{e_2 o}}{|\overrightarrow{e_1 e_2} \times \overrightarrow{e_2 o}|^2}$$

(3-2)

Let H_n be the normal components of magnetic fields at the centers of cycles, then

$$H_n = B \ E,$$

(3-3)

where B is directly calculated by (3-2).

Integrating both sides of London's equation along a cycle i,

$$\int H \cdot dS = -\oint_i \lambda_L^2 J \cdot ds$$

(3-4)

Therefore,

$$H_{n_i} S_i = -\sum_j \lambda_L^2 E_{i_j} \frac{s_{i_j}}{C_{i_j}}$$

(3-5)

where H_{n_i} is the value of H_n of cycle i, S_i is the area of cycle i, λ_L is London penetration depth, E_{i_j} is edges of cycle i, s_{i_j} is length of E_{i_j}, and C_{i_j} is the area of cross section of the block containing E_{i_j} (Fig. 3-5).

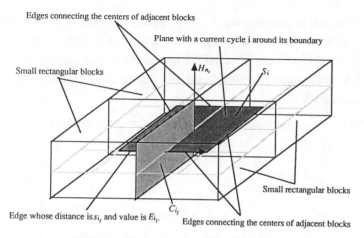

Edges connecting the centers of adjacent blocks

Plane with a current cycle i around its boundary

Small rectangular blocks

H_{n_i}

S_i

Small rectangular blocks

Edge whose distance is s_{i_j} and value is E_{i_j}.

C_{i_j}

Edges connecting the centers of adjacent blocks

Fig. 3-5 Current cycle composed of edges

Hence, H_n can be written as

$$H_n = D\ E \tag{3-6}$$

From (3-1), (3-3), (3-6), we obtain:

$$(B - D)\ A\ \begin{bmatrix} L \\ P \end{bmatrix} = 0 \tag{3-7}$$

Hence,

$$\begin{bmatrix} (B-D)A \\ 0 \quad I_d \end{bmatrix} \begin{bmatrix} L \\ P \end{bmatrix} = \begin{bmatrix} 0 \\ V \end{bmatrix}, \tag{3-8}$$

where V is the value of current paths and I_d is a uniform matrix. E can be obtained from (3-8) and (3-1) if V is given. Magnetic energy of the network is given by

$$U = \frac{\mu_0}{8\pi} \int \frac{J(r)J(r')}{|r-r'|} dr dr' + \frac{1}{2}\int \lambda_L^2 J^2 dv \tag{3-9}$$

$$= \frac{1}{2}\sum_{i,j} M_{ij}E_iE_j + \frac{1}{2}\sum \lambda_L^2 \frac{s_i}{C_i}E_i^2, \tag{3-10}$$

where μ_0 is permeability in free space, and M_{ij} is mutual inductance between current edges i and j. M_{ij} can be calculated directly by the positions of edges if $i{\neq}j$.[21] M_{ii} can be obtained by assuming that uniform current flows through a small rectangular conductor and can be computed from the shape of the conductor.[22]

If the circuit has some holes, mutual inductances between these holes can be considered.

$$U=\sum_{i,j}M_{ij}^*V_iV_j \qquad (3-11)$$

where M_{ij}^* is mutual inductance between the $i-th$ and $j-th$ holes. Therefore, if U is calculated by changing V_i's, M_{ij}^*'s are obtained.

III-IV. CAD System

Based upon the method described in Sec. III-II and III-III, a CAD system was developed for the design of superconducting inductor systems.

Pre-processing

The main task of the pre-process is transforming the structure of circuits into a current network, and choosing a minimum independent variable set. LSI patterns are specified by combinations of (basic) rectangular blocks. The planes of each rectangular block must be vertical to one of the x, y or z axes in our implementation. In this case, a rectangular block can be represented by two diagonal points. Each basic rectangular block is divided into small rectangular blocks. The centers of adjacent blocks are connected by edges, which produce a network. Independent variables, which are necessary to specify the current distribution of the network uniquely, are selected as discussed in Sec. III-II.

Inductance calculation

Simultaneous linear equation (3-8) is constructed from the results of pre-processing. (3-8) is solved by the Gaussian elimination method. Because edges are parallel to either the x, y or z axes, the first term of (3-10) is necessary only when two edges have the same direction. Inductance calculation is performed several times changing the number of divisions, if necessary. These data are used when extrapolating the results to increase the accuracy.

Post-processing

The major function of the post-processing is a display of current distribution using the results of inductance calculations. It is possible to display current distribution of a given cross section and current flow of a given plane. Current flow is a contour line of the integrated current distribution along a perpendicular path to a current path.

III-V. Example

The coupling inductance of a dc-SQUID shown in Fig. 3-6 is calculated by the CAD system described in Sec. III-IV. This dc-SQUID works as a current detector of logic signals. Two lines (an input inductor line and a dc-offset line) are mounted above a SQUID loop.

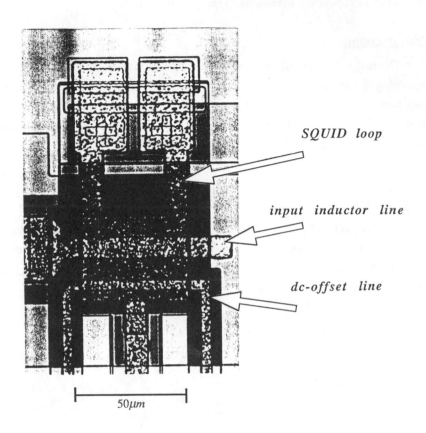

SQUID loop

input inductor line

dc-offset line

50μm

Fig. 3-6 Fabricated pattern of a dc-SQUID current detector

The mutual inductances among these two lines and the SQUID loop are calculated. The model used for the computation is shown in Fig. 3-7. The current flow of the SQUID loop is plotted in Fig. 3-8.

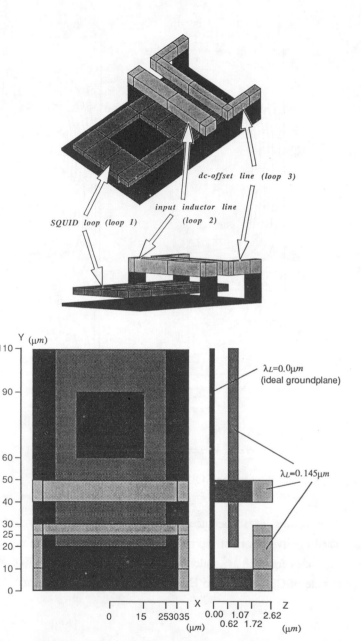

Fig. 3-7 Computational model of the dc-SQUID

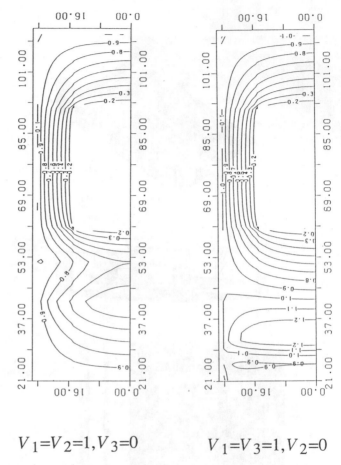

$$V_1=V_2=1, V_3=0 \qquad V_1=V_3=1, V_2=0$$

Fig. 3-8 Current flow of the SQUID loop

The results of inductance computation are shown in Table 3-1. The estimated relative errors of the results are less than 5 %. The typical number of current cycles for each M_{ij}^{*} calculation in the table is about 1500, which requires one minute of CPU-time from Hitachi's S-810 vector processor.

Table 3-1 Computational results of the SQUID inductances (pH)

M_{11}^*	M_{22}^*	M_{33}^*	M_{12}^*	M_{13}^*	M_{23}^*
9.80	11.07	23.33	0.98	0.42	0.95

The mutual inductances M_{12}^* and M_{13}^* were empirically obtained by frequency of threshold curves of the SQUID.[23] The empirical results are shown in Table 3-2. They change because of measurement and fabrication errors. Agreement between the computation and the experiment is good.

Table 3-2 Empirical results of the SQUID inductances (pH)

M_{12}^*	M_{13}^*
0.90 ~ 0.94	0.40 ~ 0.43

III-VI. Summary

We have shown the inductance calculation method for complicated three-dimensional superconducting circuits. In this method, circuits are transformed into current networks, where each edge current satisfies both London's and Maxwell's equations. A simple way to choose minimum independent variables which are necessary to specify the network uniquely is introduced. The CAD system for the superconducting inductor design was developed based upon the scheme. The coupling characteristics of the dc-SQUID was calculated using the CAD system and compared to the experimental results. Agreement between the experiment and the computation is good.

IV. Superconducting Stripline

A superconducting stripline is the most elementary inductor. Because the impedance of Josephson devices is very small, superconducting striplines are used not only for connections between superconducting circuits but also for circuit elements. This chapter discusses the properties of a superconducting stripline.

IV-I. Introduction

Because many superconducting circuits can be closely approximated by combinations of superconducting striplines, the inductance of a superconducting stripline is very important for their design.

When London penetration depth is small compared with conductor thickness, the normal component of the magnetic field on the surface of the conductor can be assumed to be 0. Using this boundary condition and Maxwell's equations and London's equations (inside the conductor), the magnetic field for the superconducting stripline shown in Fig. 4-1 is obtained.[24]

The inductance and capacitance per unit length of this stripline is

$$L = \frac{\mu_0}{K_f W} \left\{ h + \lambda_1 \coth \frac{t_1}{\lambda_1} + \lambda_2 \coth \frac{t_2}{\lambda_2} \right\} \tag{4-1}$$

$$C = \varepsilon_r \varepsilon_0 \frac{W}{h} K_f, \tag{4-2}$$

where K_f is a fringe factor shown in Fig. 4-1, λ_i is the London penetration depth of superconductor i, μ_0 and ε_0 are permeability and dielectric constant in free space, and ε_r is specific inductive capacity.

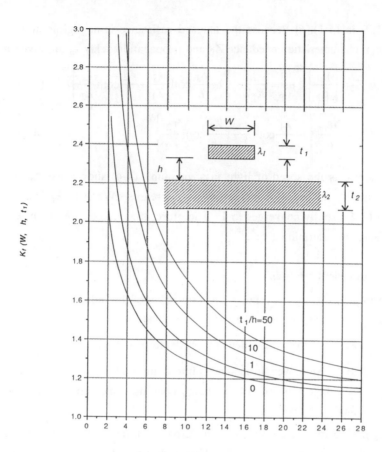

Fig. 4-1 Model and fringe factor K_f of a superconducting stripline

When current distribution changes with time, effective London penetration depth becomes a complex number and resistance is induced. In that case, a superconducting stripline can be described as a uniform transmission line whose unit impedance and admittance are given by $i\omega L^*$ and $i\omega C$, where L^* is the inductance obtained by substituting complex London penetration depth to

$\lambda_i, (i=1,2)$ in (4-1).[6] Because the induced resistance is negligible at 10 G Hz operation, characteristic impedance Z_0 and propagation delay τ_p are given by

$$Z_0 = \left[\frac{\mu_0}{\varepsilon_0}\right]^{1/2} \frac{1}{\sqrt{\varepsilon_r}} \frac{h}{K_f W} \left\{1 + \frac{\lambda_1}{h}\coth\frac{t_1}{\lambda_1} + \frac{\lambda_2}{h}\coth\frac{t_2}{\lambda_2}\right\}^{1/2} \qquad (4\text{-}3)$$

$$\tau_p = \frac{\sqrt{\varepsilon_r}}{c} \left\{1 + \frac{\lambda_1}{h}\coth\frac{t_1}{\lambda_1} + \frac{\lambda_2}{h}\coth\frac{t_2}{\lambda_2}\right\}^{1/2}, \qquad (4\text{-}4)$$

where c is the speed of light in a vacuum. (4-4) shows that τ_p becomes small when ε_r decreases, h increases or t_i increases. When $t_i > \lambda_i$ (usual case), coth in (4-4) rapidly converges to 1. Therefore, if λ_i and ε_r are given, h is the main factor in determining τ_p[*].

IV-II. Numerical analysis

Although (4-1) gives a fairly accurate value of the inductance of the superconducting stripline, the error becomes large when the thickness of the conductor is almost equal to London penetration depth or the aspect ratio $\frac{W}{h}$ becomes smaller than 1. Moreover, it becomes almost impossible to obtain an analytical solution when the complexity of boundary conditions increases. In such a case, numerical analysis is necessary.

There are four metal planes in the process currently used for the development of the QFP circuits (Fig. 4-2). The inductance of the stripline of width W and length W for all allowable metal-insulator combinations were calculated by the CAD system described in III. [**] The results are shown in Fig. 4-3.

---

[*] To decrease τ_p, h should be increased.
[**] 2D version was used.

Layer	Materials	Thickness (nm)	London penetration depth (nm)	Function
M1	Nb	200	85	Ground plane
I1a,b	SiO	300		Ground-plane isolation
R	MoN	100		Resistor
I1c	SiO	180		Resistor isolation
M2	Nb-NbN	150-100	85-278	Base electrodes
I2	SiO	320		Junction definition
M3	Pb/Au/In	450	145	Counter electrodes
I3	SiO	650		Interconnection isolation
M4	Pb/Au/In	900	145	Excitation wiring

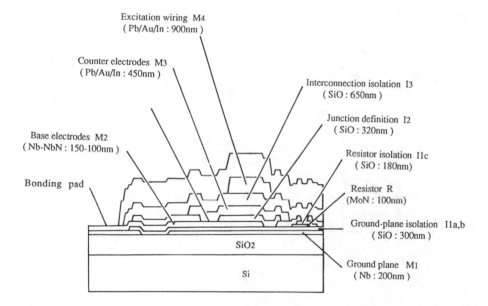

Fig. 4-2 Niobium/lead-alloy process currently used for fabrication of QFP circuits.

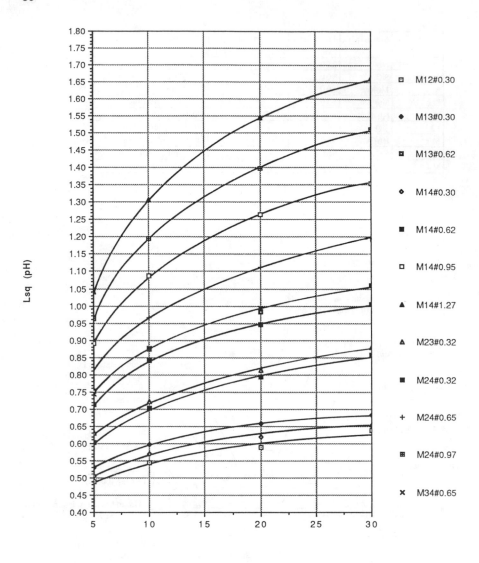

Fig. 4-3 Inductance of a superconducting stripline

$M_{ij}\#_k$ means the inductance between M_i and M_j with insulator thickness $_k\mu m$.

When W increases, the fringe effect decreases, thus increasing the square inductance.

If the groundplane is small, its fringe effect, as well as that of the stripline, should be considered. When W_g-W_s in Fig. 4-4 decreases, the inductance increases because the current inside the groundplane is restricted to a small region. This effect increases when h becomes large because the magnetic field spreads more widely when h becomes large. $L(W_g)/L(\infty)$ is shown in Fig. 4-4, where $L(W_g)$ is the inductance when the width of the groundplane is W_g.

IV-III. Two layer stripline

As shown in Fig. 4-2, the M2 layer is composed of two materials which have different London penetration depths. The following considers the superconducting striplines in which the M2 layer is used.

If the aspect ratio is large enough to neglect the fringe effect (Fig. 4-5), the magnetic field has only a y component $H_y(z)$. In that case, current distribution $J_x(z)$ is given by $-\dfrac{\partial H_y}{\partial z}$ (from (1-3)).

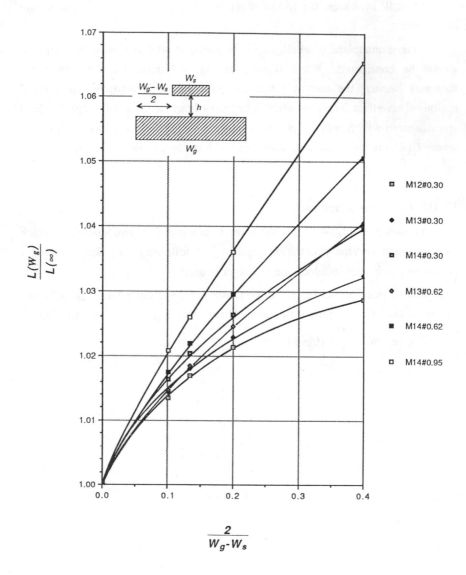

Fig. 4-4 Fringe effect of a groundplane

$M_{ij}\#_k$ means the inductance between M_i and M_j with insulator thickness $_k\mu m$.

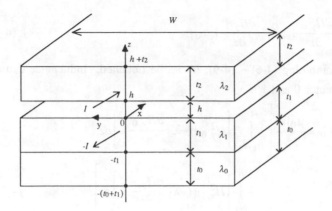

Fig. 4-5 Model of a two-layer superconducting stripline

To satisfy (1-5), H_y must satisfy

$$\frac{\partial^2 H_{y,0}}{\partial z^2} - \frac{1}{\lambda_0^2} H_{y,0} = 0 \tag{4-5-1}$$

$$\frac{\partial^2 H_{y,1}}{\partial z^2} - \frac{1}{\lambda_1^2} H_{y,1} = 0, \tag{4-5-2}$$

and

$$\frac{\partial^2 H_{y,2}}{\partial z^2} - \frac{1}{\lambda_2^2} H_{y,2} = 0, \tag{4-5-3}$$

where $H_{y,i}$ ($i=1,2,3$) is the magnetic field in the superconductor i. From the boundary condition and the restriction on the continuity of H and J,

$$H_{y,0}\,|_{z=-(t_0+t_1)} = H_{y,2}\,|_{z=h+t_2} = 0 \tag{4-6}$$

$$H_{y,1}\,|_{z=0} = H_{y,2}\,|_{z=h} = \frac{I}{W} \tag{4-7}$$

$$H_{y,0}\,|_{z=-t_1} = H_{y,1}\,|_{z=-t_1} \tag{4-8}$$

$$\frac{\partial H_{y,0}}{\partial z}\Big|_{z=-t_1}=\frac{\partial H_{y,1}}{\partial z}\Big|_{z=-t_1}.$$ (4-9)

By combining (4-6) ~ (4-9), H can be obtained. Inductance caused by the superconductor 0 and 1 is

$$L_{01}=\frac{\mu_0 W}{I^2}\left[\int_{-(t_0+t_1)}^{-t_1}\left[H_{y,0}^2+(-\lambda_0\frac{\partial H_{y,0}}{\partial z})^2\right]dz\right.$$

$$\left.+\int_{-t_1}^{0}\left[H_{y,1}^2+(-\lambda_1\frac{\partial H_{y,1}}{\partial z})^2\right]dz\right]$$ (4-10)

$$=\frac{\mu_0}{W}\left[\lambda_1\left\{1-(1+2\alpha-\alpha^2\coth\frac{t_1}{\lambda_1})e^{\frac{-2t_1}{\lambda_1}}\right\}\right.$$

$$\left.+\lambda_0(1+\alpha)^2 e^{\frac{-2t_1}{\lambda_1}}\coth\frac{t_0}{\lambda_0}\right],$$ (4-11)

where

$$\alpha=\frac{\dfrac{1}{\lambda_1}-\dfrac{1}{\lambda_0}\coth\dfrac{t_0}{\lambda_0}}{\dfrac{1}{\lambda_1}\coth\dfrac{t_1}{\lambda_1}+\dfrac{1}{\lambda_0}\coth\dfrac{t_0}{\lambda_0}}.$$ (4-12)

Inductance caused by the superconductor 2 is

$$L_2=\frac{\mu_0 W}{I^2}\left[\int_{h}^{h+t_2}\left[H_{y,2}^2+(-\lambda_0\frac{\partial H_{y,2}}{\partial z})^2\right]dz\right]$$ (4-13)

$$=\frac{\mu_0}{W}\lambda_2\coth\frac{t_2}{\lambda_2}.$$ (4-14)

Therefore, total inductance L is given by

$$L=\frac{\mu_0}{W}h+L_{01}+L_2 . \tag{4-15}$$

When $\lambda_1 \ll t_1$,

$$L_{01} \approx \frac{\mu_0}{W}\lambda_1 . \tag{4-11-1}$$

This shows that only superconductor 1 determines L_{01} if $\lambda_1 \ll t_1$ because no current flows in superconductor 0. When $t_1 \ll \lambda_1$,

$$L_{01} \approx \frac{\mu_0}{W}\lambda_0 \coth\frac{t_0}{\lambda_0} . \tag{4-11-2}$$

This shows that only superconductor 0 determines L_{01} if $t_1 \ll \lambda_1$ because the current (gradient of the magnetic field) in superconductor 1 is very small. And of course, when $\lambda=\lambda_0=\lambda_1$,

$$L_{01}=\frac{\mu_0}{W}\lambda \coth\frac{t_0+t_1}{\lambda} . \tag{4-11-3}$$

The inductances of the striplines which use the M2 layer were calculated and compared to the cases when the M2 layer is assumed to be composed of 250 nm Nb (instead of 100 nm NbN and 150nm Nb). The results are shown in table 4-1.

Table 4-1 Inductance of a 2-layer stripline

The inductance of the striplines which use the M2 layer are calculated and compared to the case when the M2 layer is assumed to be composed of niobium only.

layer		thickness (London penetration depth) (μm)			difference
1μm line	2μm line	$t_0(\lambda_0)$	$t_1(\lambda_1)$	$t_2(\lambda_0)$	(%)
M2	M1				6.1
M1	M2	0.10(0.278)	0.15(0.085)	0.20(0.085)	1.5
M3	M2				0.4
M2	M3	0.15(0.085)	0.10(0.278)	0.45(0.145)	3.6

96

When the width of the M2 layer is large, the inductance does not change whether M2 has two layers or not. This result agrees with (4-11-1) and (4-11-2). When the M2 layer is narrow, the inductance increases a little, because in that case, the current penetration into niobium-nitride decreases the fringe factor, which increases the inductance.

IV-IV. L-bend

The inductance at an L-bend corner decreases compared with that on a straight line. The inductance of the L-bend corner shown in Fig. 4-6 is calculated. The inductance of the straight line L_s is calculated from the increase of the inductance by l. The inductance of the L bend corner L_b is calculated from the total inductance and L_s. The results are summarized in Table 4-2.

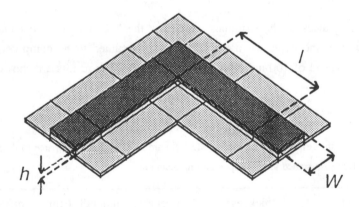

Fig. 4-6 Model of an L-bend stripline

The calculation shown in table 4-2 assumes that the thickness of the conductor is 0.45μm London penetration depth is 0.145μm and an ideal groundplane is used.

Table 4-2 Inductance of the L-bend corner

L_s is the inductance of the straight square stripline calculated from the increase in the inductance by l (almost constant when $l > W$). L_b is the inductance of the bend corner stripline calculated from L_s and the total inductance.

$W(\mu m)$	$h(\mu m)$	$\lambda_L(\mu m)$	L_s (pH)	L_b (pH)	$\dfrac{L_r}{L_s}$
5	0.32	0.085	0.47	0.37	0.79
10	0.32	0.085	0.60	0.47	0.78
5	0.62	0.085	0.70	0.55	0.79
5	0.32	0.145	0.52	0.41	0.79
10	0.32	0.145	0.64	0.50	0.78
5	0.62	0.145	0.75	0.59	0.80

In this model, the ratio of L_b and L_s is almost constant, independently of W and h and λ_L.

If the capacitance of the L-bend corner does not change from that of the straight stripline, the characteristic impedance of the L-bend corner is $\sqrt{0.8} Z_0$ where Z_0 is the characteristic impedance of a straight stripline. Therefore the reflection ratio ρ at the L-bend corner is

$$\rho = \frac{1-\sqrt{0.8}}{1+\sqrt{0.8}} = 0.06 \ . \tag{4-16}$$

IV-V. Summary

This chapter discussed the properties of superconducting striplines. The inductances of superconducting striplines for the process currently used were obtained. The effects of using two materials in one conductor layer, as well as impedance mismatch at the L-bend corner, were discussed. These data are used in our laboratory for the design of superconducting circuits.

V. Inductance of a square washer coil whose slit is not covered

A study is made into the coupling characteristics of a square washer coil whose slit is not covered. The self inductances of a washer coil and an input coil, as well as the mutual inductance between them, are calculated numerically. Some useful equations are derived by analyzing the results.

V-I. Introduction

A planar coupled dc SQUID design which uses a square washer coil has become very common.[12] This kind of dc-SQUIDs uses a transformer composed of a square washer coil and a multi-turn input coil (Fig. 5-1). When IBM developed it at first time, the slit of the washer coil is covered by a conductor in order to reduce the leakage flux from the slit. Recently, many designers use the washer coil whose slit is not covered because of its simplicity.[*]

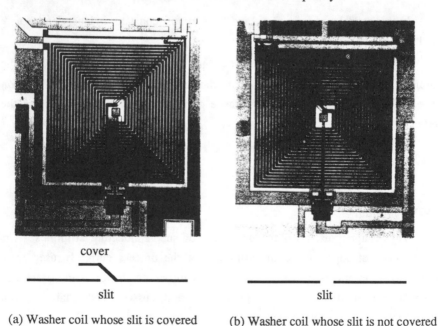

(a) Washer coil whose slit is covered   (b) Washer coil whose slit is not covered

Fig. 5-1 Square washer coil of a dc-SQUID
The cross sections of the slits are also drawn. The input coils are omitted.

---

* Sometimes, the slit is used to pass the return of the input coil. In this case, only two metal layers are required for making the washer transformer.

If the square washer coil has a cover over the slit, it is well approximated by an isolated hole. In that case, the self inductance of the square washer (L_1) and an input coil (L_2), and the mutual inductance between two coils (M) are given by the following equations:[8, 11]

$$L_1=1.25\mu_0 d \quad (W \gg d) \tag{5-1}$$

$$M=nL_1 \tag{5-2}$$

$$L_2=L_s+n^2 L_1, \tag{5-3}$$

where W is the width of the square washer, d is the length of its hole, n is the number of turns of the input coil, and L_s is the inductance of the stripline composed of the input coil and the square washer coil.[**]

However, if the slit of the washer coil is not covered, these inductances increase because of the inductance of the slit, and the above equations cannot be used.

In this chapter, L_1, L_2, and M are calculated numerically for models of three-dimensional square washer transformers, shown in Fig. 5-2, by changing structural parameters.[21, 25] Some useful equations which replace (5-1)-(5-3) are obtained by analyzing the results.

[**] When the shape of the hole is a circle, its self inductance is given by $\mu_0 d$, where d is the diameter of the hole. It is interesting that the coefficient of (5-1) is equal to the area ratio of the circle and the square, i.e., $1.25=4/\pi$.

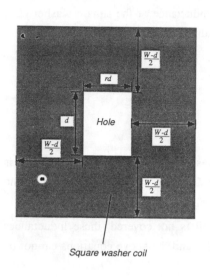

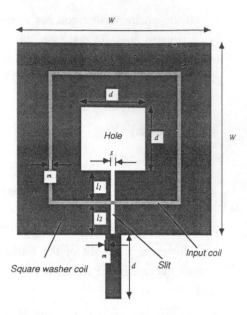

(a) Computational model of a washer coil whose slit is covered

(b) Computational model of a washer coil whose slit is not covered

Fig. 5-2 Three dimensional computational models of square washer transformers

(a) A model of a square washer coil whose slit is covered. The thickness of the conductor is 0.2μm, effective London penetration depth is 0.085μm and d=25μm.

(b) A model of a square washer transformer whose slit is not covered. The thickness of the conductors and the insulator between them are 0.2μm and 0.3μm respectively. London penetration depth is 0.085μm, m=2.5μm and d=25μm. A groundplane is attached over the connecting part outside the slit to reduce the influence of this part.

V-II. Self inductance of a washer coil whose slit is covered

The self inductance of the square washer coil shown in Fig. 5-2-(a) is calculated by changing r and W.[***]

[***] In our model, the inductance caused by the kinetic energy of super-electrons is very small (usually less than 1%). Therefore, this result can be applied even when the London penetration depth differs from our case, if it is smaller than the thickness of the conductor.

The results of the calculation are shown in Fig. 5-3.

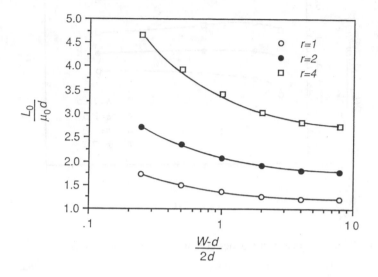

Fig. 5-3 Self inductance of a washer coil whose slit is covered
The inductance reaches almost constant when $W \approx max(d,rd)$.

The inductance becomes almost constant when W reaches the order of $max(d,rd)$. If $W \gg rd$ and $W \gg d$, the inductance is given, within 5% error in the range of $1/4 \leq r \leq 4$, by

$$L_0 = (0.63r + 0.54)\mu_0 d. \qquad (5\text{-}4)$$

(5-4) is an extended form of (5-1). It can be rewritten using the perimeter of the hole $p = 2(r+1)d$ as $L_0 \approx 0.3\mu_0 p$, which is accurate within 10% error.

V-III. Self inductance of a washer coil whose slit is not covered

When the self inductance of the square washer coil shown in Fig. 5-2-(b) is calculated, the inductance increases relative to a square washer coil whose slit is covered because of the leakage inductance caused by the slit. The increase in inductance per unit length is shown in Fig. 5-4.

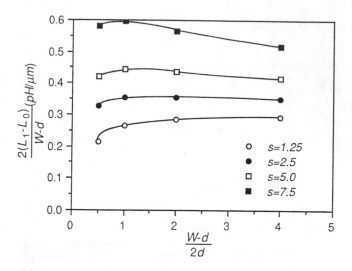

Fig. 5-4 Self inductance of a washer coil whose slit is not covered

The increase of the inductance in comparison with Fig. 5-3 is shown. It is almost equal to (5-5) if $W \gg d \gg s$.

From the results of the computation, I found that the current distribution of the washer coil with an uncovered slit is almost the same as that of the washer coil with a covered slit, except for the component parallel to the slit in the region near the slit. Therefore, when $w \gg d \gg s$, the increase in inductance caused by the slit is given by the inductance of the structure shown in Fig. 5-5, which is given by

$$L_\Delta = \mu_0 \frac{K(s/W)}{K'(s/W)} \, , \tag{5-5}$$

where K is the complete elliptic integral of the first kind, and K' is a complement function of K.

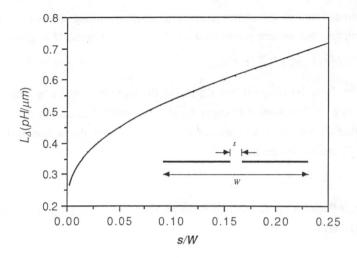

Fig. 5-5 Inductance of two parallel thin plates with reverse current

The inductance of the structure shown can be calculated analytically. When $s \ll W$, s/W has weak dependency on W. Therefore, the inductance has weak dependency on W if $s \ll W$.

For our model, L_Δ is accurate within 5% error when $W/d=4, s/W \le 0.01$, and within 10% error when $W/d=4, s/W \le 0.02$. Thus, when $W \gg d \gg s$, L_1 is given by

$$L_1 = L_0 + L_\Delta(W-d)/2. \qquad (5\text{-}6)$$

V-IV. Mutual inductance between a washer coil and an input coil

The mutual inductance between a washer coil and an input coil (M) is given by the flux of the washer coil when unit current flows in the input coil. Therefore, when the current of the input coil is well imaged in the square washer coil, M is given by the flux caused by the unit mirror current in the square washer coil. If the slit of the square washer coil is covered, M is determined mainly by L_1 independently of the position of an input coil, because almost all flux is caused by the mirror current along the hole. When the slit is

104

not covered, some of the mirror current $(1-c)$ flows along the slit outside the input coil, and that current produces the leakage flux. Hence, M is given by

$$M=c(L_0+L_\Delta l_1)-(1-c)L_\Delta, \qquad (5\text{-}7)$$

where l_1 is the length of the slit inside the input coil, and c is a function of the structure. (Therefore, c changes by the position of the input coil.) When $c\approx1$, (when $l_1\approx(W-d)/2$ and almost all mirror current flows inside the input coil), (5-7) can be written as

$$M=L_0+L_\Delta l_1, \qquad (5\text{-}7)'$$

Fig. 5-6 shows the relation between M and l_1 which is obtained by numerical calulations.

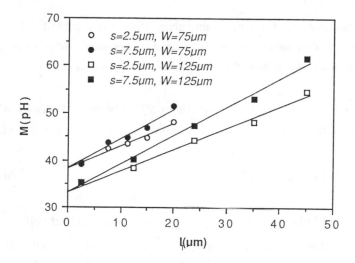

Fig. 5-6 Mutual inductance between a washer coil and an input coil

If (5-7)' is applied for the structure used in Fig. 5-6, the result is accurate within 5% error when $l_1\geq(W-d)/4$, but the error becomes about 15% when $(W-d)/4>l_1$.

M can be easily and precisely measured by the period of the flux modulation of dc-SQUIDs. Table 5-1 shows the experimental results of M and the values of (5-2) and (5-7)'.

Table 5-1 Experimental results of M

W (μm)	d (μm)	s (μm)	l_1 (μm)	n	(5-2) (pH)	(5-7) (pH)	Experiment (pH)
475	25	5	210	1	39	109	105
275	25	5	110	1	39	79	71

V-V. Self inductance of an input coil

A transformer composed of self inductance L_1, L_2 and mutual inductance M can be transformed into the series connection of (a) the shunt inductance L_1 of the primary turn, (b) the ideal transformer with turn ratio $1:M/L_1$, and (c) the leakage inductance $L_2(1-M^2/(L_1 L_2))$ of the secondary turn. Hence, the leakage inductance (c) is given by the inductance of the secondary coil when the primary coil is shorted. If the slit is covered, the leakage inductance is almost equal to the self inductance of the stripline which is composed of the input coil and the square washer coil (L_s). However, if the slit is not covered, the leakage inductance increases because the current avoids the slit by flowing parallel to and around it. The increase in the inductance caused by the detour of the current is $L_\Delta l_2$ when $W >> d >> s$. Therefore, L_2 is written as

$$L_2 = (M/L_1)^2 L_1 + L_s + L_\Delta l_2 \qquad (5\text{-}8)$$

In our model, (5-8) is accurate within 10% error.

V-VI. Multi-turn input coil

Because (5-6) [L_1] is almost independent of the existence of the input coil, it is satisfied in the case of multi-turn input coil. However, some modifications are required to (5-7) [M] and (5-8) [L_2] when the input coil is multi-winding.

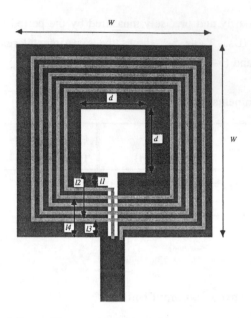

Fig. 5-7 Multi-turn input coil

If the input coil is n-turn winding and the distance from each winding to the edge of the central hole is given by (5-9-1), M can be written as (5-10) by using (5-7)'.

$$l_i = l_1 + (i-1)/(n-1)(l_2 - l_1) \tag{5-9-1}$$

$$M = \sum_{i=1}^{n}(L_0 + L_\Delta l_i) = n(L_0 + L_\Delta \frac{l_1 + l_2}{2}) \tag{5-10}$$

Table 5-2 shows the experimental results of M for multi-turn input coils. It also shows the values of (5-2) and (5-10). Because the error of (5-7)' becomes large when l_1 is small, actual M is smaller than (5-10) (but larger than (5-2)). More rigorous calculations (instead of (5-10)) may be required when l_i is small.

Table 5-2 Experimental results of M for multi-turn input coils

W	d	s	l_1	l_2	n	(5-2)	(5-10)	Experiment
(μm)	(μm)	(μm)	(μm)	(μm)		(pH)	(pH)	(pH)
475	25	5	10	240	20	780	1620	1100
275	25	5	10	110	10	390	610	440

When (5-9-2) gives the distance from each winding to the outer edge of the washer coil, L_2 can be written as (5-11) by using (5-8).

$$l_j = l_3 + (j-1)/(n-1)(l_4 - l_3) \tag{5-9-2}$$

$$L_2 = (M/L_1)^2 L_1 + L_s + nL_\Delta \frac{l_3 + l_4}{2} \tag{5-11}$$

V-VII. Summary

I have studied the inductance of a square washer SQUID having an uncovered slit. The increase of L_1 caused by the slit is given by (5-5) when $W \gg d \gg s$. M has dependency on l_1 which is given by (5-7). The leakage inductance of L_2 increases because of the detour of the current near the slit, which is given by $L_\Delta l_2$.

VI. Superconducting transformer

Transformers are used for the activation and the Input/Output of QFP's. Many useful functions including signal negation and impedance conversion of QFP signals can be easily done by transformers. Signal negation is a difficult function in conventional JJ devices, but it is easily achieved by an inverting transformer in QFP circuits. The impedance conversion is required when a QFP drives the load at a long distance, because the wiring inductance itself is a load of the QFP, and that inductance cannot be too large for the stable operation of a QFP. The impedance conversion can also be done by using a multi-turn transformer. This chapter discusses various kinds of superconducting transformers for the QFP circuits.

VI-I. Introduction

The QFP (Quantum Flux Parametron) is a new cryogenic switching device based on the parametron principle and Josephson technology.[13, 14, 15, 16] It is expected to achieve high gain, high-speed operation, with low power dissipation. The circuit diagram and structure of the QFP are shown in Fig. 6-1.

When the circuit is excited, the current in the left and right loops flow in reverse as shown in Fig. 6-1. When each excitation flux is π and the flux of each excited inductor is ϕ_1 and the flux of the load inductor is ϕ_2, the flux of each Josephson junction becomes $\pi-(\phi_1+\phi_2)$ due to the flux quantization. Therefore,

$$I=I_m\sin(\pi-(\phi_1+\phi_2))=I_m\sin(\phi_1+\phi_2) \tag{6-1}$$

$$\phi_1=\frac{2\pi}{\Phi_0}L_1I \tag{6-2}$$

and

$$\phi_2=\frac{2\pi}{\Phi_0}L_2I . \tag{6-3}$$

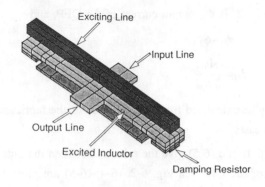

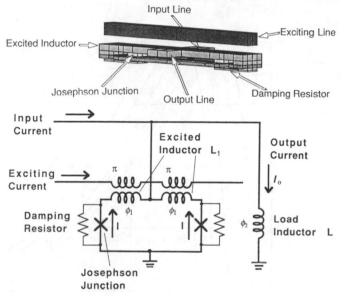

Fig. 6-1 Structure and circuit diagram of the QFP

From (6-1),(6-2) and (6-3),

$$\frac{I_o}{I_m} = 2\sin\phi \qquad (6\text{-}4)$$

and

$$L = \frac{1}{2}(L_J \frac{\phi}{\sin\phi} - L_1), \qquad (6\text{-}5)$$

where $I_o=2I$ is the output current of the QFP, and

$$\phi=\phi_1+\phi_2 \tag{6-6}$$

$$L_J=\frac{\Phi_0}{2\pi I_m} \, . \tag{6-7}$$

L_1 can be calculated from the structure of the fabricated pattern, and $L_1=1.37pH$ in our case.

(6-4) and (6-5) give the relation between the output current and load inductance of the QFP. In Fig. 6-2, (6-4)-(6-5) are plotted and the results of fundamental experiments are shown.[26]

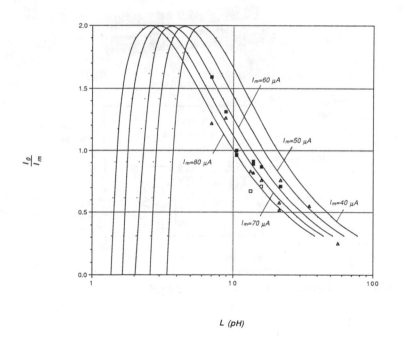

Fig. 6-2 Relation between output current and load of the QFP

When $I_m=50\mu A$, I_o has a maximum at $L=5pH$. This load condition should be used for the stable QFP operations. Because the wiring inductance itself is a load of the QFP, the wiring cannot be so long in order to satisfy this load condition. Therefore, impedance conversion by a transformer is necessary for increasing the load drivability of a QFP. This is one of important functions of transformers in QFP circuits.

Another important function of a transformer is the linear transformation of QFP outputs. For example, addition/subtraction of two QFP outputs can be easily made by a transformer called H_2, and signal negation can be naturally done by an inverting transformer.

As stated above, transformers are very important parts in QFP circuits. In the following sections, several properties of transformers will be discussed.

VI-II. Coupling scheme

Any single-input (primary) single-output (secondary) inductance network can be specified by the inductance matrix, i.e.,

$$\begin{bmatrix} F_1 \\ F_2 \end{bmatrix} = \begin{bmatrix} L_1 & -M \\ M & -L_2 \end{bmatrix} \begin{bmatrix} I_1 \\ I_2 \end{bmatrix} \tag{6-8}$$

where F_i, I_i ($i=1,2$) are flux and current of primary ($i=1$) and secondary ($i=2$) windings, L_i ($i=1,2$) is the self inductance of primary ($i=1$) and secondary ($i=2$) windings, and M is the mutual inductance between them.

(6-8) can be transformed as follows:

$$\begin{bmatrix} F_1 \\ I_1 \end{bmatrix} = \begin{bmatrix} L_1/M & (L_1L_2-M^2)/M \\ 1/M & L_2/M \end{bmatrix} \begin{bmatrix} F_2 \\ I_2 \end{bmatrix}$$

$$= \begin{bmatrix} 1 & 0 \\ 1/L_1 & 1 \end{bmatrix} \begin{bmatrix} L_1/M & 0 \\ 0 & M/L_1 \end{bmatrix}$$

$$\begin{bmatrix} 1 & L_2(1-M^2/(L_1L_2)) \\ 0 & 1 \end{bmatrix} \begin{bmatrix} F_2 \\ I_2 \end{bmatrix}. \tag{6-9}$$

This means that the transformer specified by (6-8) can be transformed into a series connection of (a) a shunt inductance L_1 of the primary turn, (b) an ideal transformer with turn ratio $1:M/L_1$, and (c) a leakage inductance $L_2(1-M^2/(L_1L_2))$ of the secondary turn (Fig. 6-3).

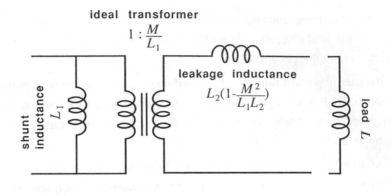

PRIMARY COIL   **SECONDARY COIL**

Fig. 6-3 Equivalent circuit of transformer

Hence, coupling constant k is given by

$$k^2 = \frac{M^2}{L_1 L_2} = \frac{1}{1 + \dfrac{L_l}{n^2 L_1}}, \tag{6-10}$$

where n and L_l are given by

$$n = M/L_1 = k \left[L_2/L_1 \right]^{1/2} \tag{6-11}$$

$$L_l = L_2 (1 - M^2/(L_1 L_2)) = L_2 k'^2, \tag{6-12}$$

where $k'(>0)$ is the complementary coupling constant defined by

$$k'^2 = 1 - k^2 . \tag{6-13}$$

When the secondary coil is mounted on the primary coil, and the current of the secondary coil is well imaged in the primary winding, n becomes an integer and is given by the winding ratio. The leakage inductance L_l is the inductance of the secondary winding when the primary winding is shorted. Therefore, L_l is given by the inductance of a stripline composed of the primary and the secondary windings.

(6-10) shows that $\dfrac{L_l}{n^2 L_1}$ must be minimized in order to increase k. Some coupling schemes are shown in Fig. 6-4. $L_l/(n^2L_1)$ values for each winding are listed in Table 6-1.

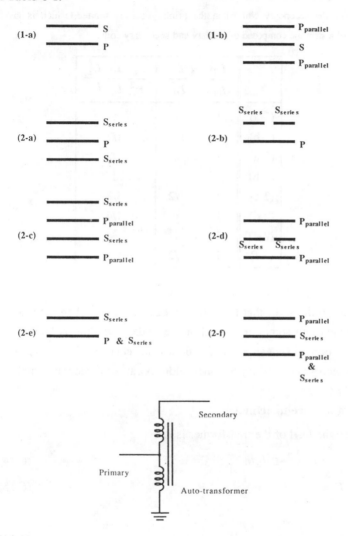

Fig. 6-4 Coupling schemes

P and S denote primary and secondary windings respectively. Subscripts *parallel* and *series* indicate that the primary or secondary windings are connected in parallel or in series. An auto-transformer is used in (2-e) and (2-d).

Table 6-1 $L_l/(n^2 L_1)$

L_1^* and L_l^* are L_1 and L_l of the transformer (1-a). The leakage inductance L_l is given by the inductance of the secondary coil when the primary coil is shorted, which is given by the inductance of a stripline composed of primary and secondary coils.

	$\dfrac{L_1}{L_1^*}$	$\dfrac{L_l}{L_l^*}$	$\dfrac{1}{n^2}\dfrac{L_l}{L_l^*}\dfrac{L_1^*}{L_1}$
(1-a)	1	1	1
(1-b)	1	1/2	1/2
(2-a)	1	2	1/2
(2-b)	1	4	1
(2-c)	1	3/2	3/8
(2-d)	1	1	1/4
(2-e)	1	1	1/4
(2-f)	1	1/2	1/8

These results show that the coupling becomes tight when the primary winding is divided into some pieces and the secondary winding is laid among them, because L_l becomes small while L_1 dones not change.[*] Moreover, k increases when the secondary winding becomes wider because L_l becomes small.

VI-III. Impedance matching

When the load of the transformer is L,

$$F_1=(L_2k'^2+L)I_2/n \tag{6-14}$$

$$F_2=LI_2 \tag{6-15}$$

and

$$I_1=nI_2+F_1/L_1 \ . \tag{6-16}$$

---

[*] These coupling schemes require good planarization technique.

From (6-14), (6-15) and (6-16)

$$\frac{I_2}{I_1} = \frac{1}{n} \frac{L_2 k^2}{L_2 + L} \tag{6-17}$$

$$\frac{F_2}{F_1} = \frac{n}{1 + \frac{L_2}{L} k'^2} \ . \tag{6-18}$$

Therefore, energy transfer efficiency is

$$\frac{E_2}{E_1} = \frac{F_2 I_2}{F_1 I_1}$$

$$= \frac{k^2}{1 + k'^2 + L/L_2 + L_2/Lk'^2} \tag{6-19}$$

$$\leq \left(\frac{k}{1 + k'} \right)^2 , \tag{6-20}$$

where the maximum value of (6-19) is given when $L = L_2 k'$. This is the condition of impedance matching. In Fig. 6-5, E_2/E_1 is shown when $L = mL_2$ and when the impedance is matched.

$L_2 k'$ can be considered as the value of the load which can be driven by the transformer, and is given by

$$L_2 k' = \left(\frac{k'}{k} \right)^2 n^2 L_1 \ . \tag{6-21}$$

Hence, if the turn ratio n is increased, more loads can be driven.

116

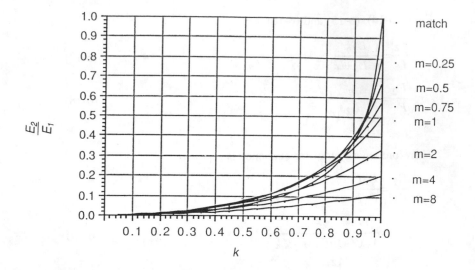

Fig. 6-5 Energy transfer efficiency

Energy transfer efficiency when $L=L_2k'$ and when $L=mL_2$.

From (6-16), (6-17) and (6-11), the impedance of the primary coil L^* is given by

$$L^*=\frac{F_1}{I_1}=\frac{L+L_2k'^2}{L+L_2}\frac{L_2k^2}{n^2}\ .$$ (6-22)

Therefore,

$$L_2=\frac{(\frac{n}{k})^2L^*-L+\left\{((\frac{n}{k})^2L^*-L)^2+4(k'\frac{n}{k})^2LL^*\right\}^{1/2}}{2k'^2}$$ (6-23)

and

$$L_1=(k/n)^2L_2\ .$$ (6-24)

L_1,L_2 can be calculated from (6-23) and (6-24) if n,k,L^* and L are given.

When $L=L_2k'$ (impedance matching),

$$L_2|_{L=L_{match}}=(n/k)^2L^*/k' \qquad (6\text{-}25)$$

and

$$L_1|_{L=L_{match}}=L^*/k' \qquad (6\text{-}26)$$

where

$$L_{match}=L_2k'=(n/k)^2L^* . \qquad (6\text{-}27)$$

If L^* is chosen such that the output current of the QFP is maximized,

$$L^*\approx\frac{\pi}{2}L_J=10pH. \qquad (6\text{-}28)$$

(6-26) and (6-27) are plotted in Fig. 6-6.

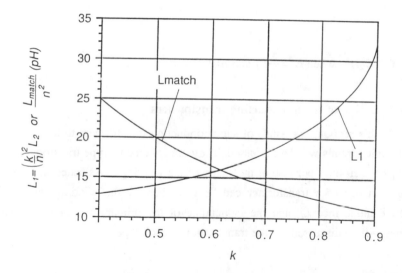

Fig. 6-6 L_{match}/n^2 and $L_1=(\frac{k}{n})^2 L_2$ when $L=L_{match}$ and $L^*=\frac{\pi}{2}L_J$

The energy transfer efficiency is obtained from (6-19) and (6-23) as a function of L, and this is plotted in Fig. 6-7. The value of L which maximizes the

118

curve of Fig. 6-7 is given by (6-27).

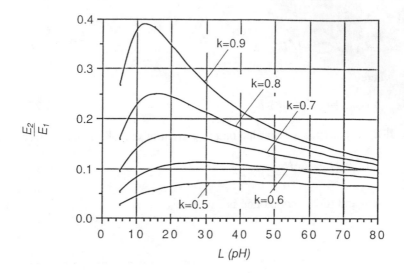

Fig. 6-7 E_2/E_1 when $L^*=\frac{\pi}{2}L_J$ and $n=1$

VI-IV. Design of superconducting transformers

In this section, two kinds of superconducting transformers to be used in the QFP logic circuits will be discussed. They are called an I-type transformer and a U-type transformer because of the shape of the windings. As stated in VI-II, the characteristics of a transformer can be described by the winding ratio n, the leakage inductance L_l, and the inductance of the primary winding L_1. These values will be discussed for the transformer of each type.

VI-IV-I. I-type transformer

Coupling constant k becomes large if there is no groundplane around the coupling part, because L_1 becomes large while L_l does not change. The following considers the superconducting transformer called an I-type transformer whose coupling part has no groundplane (Fig. 6-8).

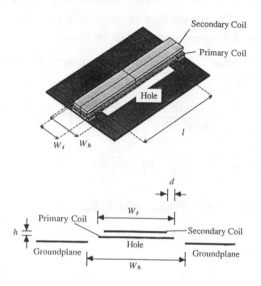

Fig. 6-8 Structure of an I-type transformer

If $W_h, W_s \gg h$ and the current in the secondary coil is well imaged in the primary coil, then $n \approx 1$.

In this case, L_l is given by the inductance of the stripline composed of the primary and secondary windings.

$$L_l = \frac{\mu_0 h l}{W_s - 2d}. \tag{6-29}$$

Because the structure of the primary winding is complicated, the inductance of the primary coil cannot be obtained analytically. Numerical calculations using the CAD system described in III were made for the model shown in Fig. 6-8. The results of the computations indicate that the inductance of the primary coil is closely approximated by

$$L_1 = \mu_0 \left\{ \frac{K'(W_s/W_h)}{4K(W_s/W_h)} l + 0.12(W_h - W_s) \right\}, \tag{6-30}$$

if $l \geq W_h$ (within 10 % error).

The first term of (6-30) is the unit inductance in the l direction of this structure when $l=\infty$. The second term is the inductance induced by the current in the W_h direction. It is almost independent of l.

(6-10) indicates that L_1/L_l should be maximized in order to increase k. From (6-29) and (6-30),

$$\frac{L_1}{L_l} = \frac{W_s - 2d}{h} \left\{ \frac{K'(W_s/W_h)}{4K(W_s/W_h)} + 0.12 \frac{W_h - W_s}{l} \right\}$$

$$= \frac{W_h}{h} (a - \frac{2d}{W_h})(\frac{K'(a)}{4K(a)} + 0.12 \frac{1-a}{b}), \tag{6-31}$$

where $W_s = aW_h$, $l = bW_h$. Therefore, if $W_s \gg 2d$,

$$f = \frac{K'(a)a}{4K(a)} + 0.12 \frac{a(1-a)}{b} \tag{6-32}$$

should be maximized. f becomes almost flat around its maximum point. The value of a for maximum f is almost independent of b, and is given by

$$a \approx 0.7 . \tag{6-33}$$

If $b > 2$, $f \approx 0.18$ and

$$k^2 = \frac{1}{1 + \dfrac{h}{0.18 W_h}} . \tag{6-34}$$

VI-IV-II. U-type transformer

Because an I-type transformer has an isolated hole in the groundplane, the probability of flux pinning during heat cycles becomes large. If the flux is trapped in the hole, superconducting loop current is induced around the hole, which may cause erroneous circuit operations. To alleviate the influence of flux pinning, some mechanism such as a moat should be used.[27]

The following considers the trap-immune transformer called a U-type transformer which has a slit instead of a hole in the groundplane. (Fig. 6-9) Because the U-type transformer has no superconducting loop, the probability of flux pinning is small compared to the I-type transformer. *

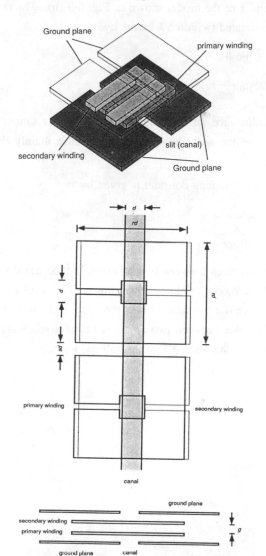

Fig. 6-9 Structure and computational model of the U-type transformer

---

* However, a slit has no superconducting shielding effect, the transformer may sense the ambient field. This can be

The inductances of the transformer were calculated by the CAD system changing d, r, and g of the model shown in Fig. 6-9 (b). The results show that it is closely approximated (within 5% error) by

$$L_1 = 1.25\mu_0 d, \tag{6-35}$$

$$L_l = 1.25\mu_0 \frac{g}{\log} r. \tag{6-36}$$

The self inductance of the primary winding L_1 is almost independent of r or the existence of the secondary winding, and it is mainly determined by the size of the hole.

Therefore, the coupling constant is given by

$$k^2 = \frac{1}{1 + \dfrac{g}{d \log r}}. \tag{6-37}$$

Mutual inductances between two adjacent U-type transformers were calculated for the same model ($r=1$) by changing s. The results are summarized in Fig. 6-10, which shows the ratio of self inductance of the primary winding and the mutual inductance between two adjacent primary windings. When $s=1$, the mutual inductance is less than 3% of the self inductance.

---

avoided by using two U-type transformers which are connected to cancel the ambient field. The transformer of this type is called an E-type transformer.

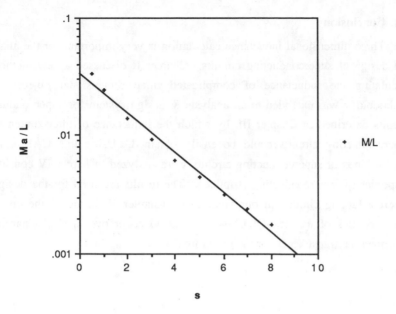

Fig. 6-10 Adjacent coupling of the U-type transformers

VI-V. Summary

This chapter described the transformers for the QFP circuits. The relation between the structure and the coupling constant as well as the relation between the load and the energy transfer efficiency were discussed. If the inductance of the primary winding is obtained, the structure of the transformer can be determined from calculations. The inductances of the primary windings of an I-type and a U-type transformer were obtained using the CAD system described in III.

VII. Conclusion

Three-dimensional inductance calculation is very important for the analysis and design of superconducting circuits. Chapter II discussed a new method of calculating the inductance of complicated three dimensional objects. The methodology was extended to an analysis & design system for superconducting circuits described in Chapter III, by which the inductance of three dimensional superconducting circuits could be easily obtained. Using this CAD system, several kinds of superconducting circuits were analyzed. Chapter IV considered properties of superconducting striplines. The results are used for the design of superconducting circuits in our laboratory. Chapter V discussed the coupling characteristics of the dc SQUID which had no cover over a slit. Chapter VI described the transformer for the QFP circuits.

References

1. H. K. Onnes, *Comm. Leiden Suppl.*, vol. 58, p. 16, 1924.

2. W. Meissner and R. Ochsenfeld, *Naturwissenshaften*, vol. 21, p. 787, 1933.

3. F. London and H. London, *Proc. Roy. Soc.*, vol. A 149, p. 71, 1935.

4. V. L. Ginzburg and L. D. Landau, "On the theory of superconductivity (in Russian)," *Zh. Eksp. Teor. Fiz.*, p. 1064, 1950.

5. J. Bardeen, L. N. Cooper, and J. R. Schrieffer, "Theory of superconductivity," *Phys. Rev.*, vol. 108, p. 1174, 1957.

6. H. Hayakawa, et. al, *Ultra-high speed Josephson devices*, Baifu-kan, Tokyo, Japan, 1986.

7. N. Shimizu, Y. Harada, N. Miyamoto, and E. Goto, "A New A/D Converter with Quantum Flux Parametron," *IEEE Trans. Magn.*, vol. MAG-25, to be published.

8. M. B. Ketchen and J. M. Jaycox, "Ultra-low-noise tunnel junction SQUID with a tightly coupled planar input coil," *Appl. Phys. Lett.*, vol. 40, no. 8, pp. 736-738, Apr. 1982.

9. C. A. Hamilton and F. L. Lloyd, "A 10-V Josephson Voltage Standard," *IEEE Tran. Magn.*, vol. MAG-25, to be publised.

10. D. E. McCumber, *J. Appl. Phys.*, vol. 39, no. 7, p. 3113, 1968.

11. M. B. Ketchen and J. M. Jaycox, "Planar coupling scheme for ultra low noise dc SQUIDs," *IEEE Trans. Magn.*, vol. MAG-17, no. 1, pp. 400-403, Jan. 1981.

12. M. B. Ketchen, "Integrated thin-film dc SQUID sensors," *IEEE Trans. Magn.*, vol. MAG-23, no. 2, pp. 1650-1657, Mar. 1987.

13. K. F. Loe and E. Goto, "Analysis of Flux Input and Output Josephson Pairs Device," *IEEE Trans. Magn.*, vol. MAG-21, no. 2, pp. 884-887, 1985.

14. E. Goto and K. F. Loe, *DC Flux Parametron,* World Scientific, Singapore, 1986.

15. Yutaka Harada, Hideaki Nakane, Nobuo Miyamoto, Ushio Kawabe, Eiichi Goto, and Takashi Soma, "Basic Operations of the Quantum Flux Parametron," *IEEE Trans. Magn.*, vol. MAG-23, no. 5, pp. 3801-3807, September 1987.

16. Yutaka Harada, Eiichi Goto, and Nobuo Miyamoto, *Quantum Flux Parametron*, pp. 389-392, December 1987.

17. L. E. Alsop, A. S. Goodman, F. G. Gustavson, and W. L. Miranker, "A Numerical Solution of a Model for a Superconductor Field Problem," *J. Comput. Phys.*, vol. 31, pp. 216-239, 1979.

18. W. H. Chang, "Numerical Calculation of the Inductance of a Multi-superconductor Transmission Line System," *IEEE Trans. Magn.*, vol. MAG-17, no. 1, pp. 764-766, Jan. 1981.

19. P. A. Brennan, N. Raver, and A. E. Ruehli, "Three-Dimensional Inductance Computations with Partial Element Equivalent Circuits," *IBM J. Res. Develop.*, vol. 23, no. 6, pp. 661-668, Nov. 1979.

20. K. Nishi and S. Yamamoto, "Measurement of 3D model inductance," in *Proceedings of the Third Riken Symposium on Josephson Electronics (in Japanese), Wako-shi, Japan, 1986*, ed. T. Soma, et al., pp. 49-52, Wako-shi, Japan, Mar. 1986.

21. M. Hosoya, E. Goto, and T. Soma, "Extrapolated Boundary Element Method for Three Dimensional Inductance Calculation," *J. Comput. Phys.*, vol. 74, pp. 94-109, 1988.

22. A. E. Ruehli, "Inductance Calculations in a Complex Integrated Circuit Environment," *IBM J. Res. Develop.*, vol. 16, pp. 470-481, Sep. 1972.

23. W. H. Chang, "Measurment and Calculation of Josephson Junction Device Inductances," *J. Appl. Phys.*, vol. 52, no. 3, pp. 1417-1426, Mar. 1981.

24. W. H. Chang, "The Inductance of a superconducting strip transmission line," *J. Appl. Phys.*, vol. 50, no. 12, pp. 8129-8134, Dec. 1980.

25. M. Hosoya, E. Goto, N. Shimizu, Y. Harada, and N. Miyamoto, "Inductance calculation system for superconducting circuits," *IEEE Trans. Magn.*, vol. MAG-25, to be published.

26. N. Shimizu, Y. Harada, N. Miyamoto, M. Hosoya, and E. Goto, "Fundamental characteristics of the QFP measured by the dc SQUID," *IEEE Trans. Electron Devices*, to be published.

27. Stuart Bermon and Tushar Gheewala, "Moat-Guarded Josephson SQUIDs," *IEEE Trans. Magn.*, vol. MAG-19, no. 3, pp. 1160-1164, May 1983.

128

X-I. Analytical solutions of the inductances for some structures

In the following, the inductances of some two-dimensional structures are obtained analytically.

The conformal mapping (X1-1) maps z-plane to ω-plane as shown in Fig. X1-1.

$$\omega = \int_0^z \frac{dz}{\sqrt{(1-z^2)(1-k^2z^2)}} \tag{X1-1}$$

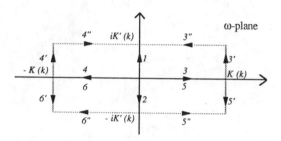

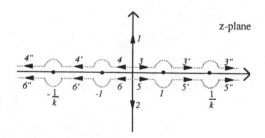

Fig. X1-1. Conformal mapping of (X1-1)

The magnetic field of Fig. X1-2-(a) is given by

$$H = \frac{i}{\sqrt{(1-z^2)(1-k^2z^2)}} \tag{X1-2}$$

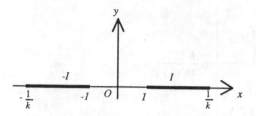

Fig. X1-2 (a) Parallel thin plates

Therefore, the inductance per unit length is given by

$$L=\mu \left| \frac{\int_{-43} Hdz}{\int_{-3'5'} Hdz} \right| =\mu \frac{K(k)}{K(k')}$$ (X1-3)

The magnetic field of Fig. X1-2-(b) $(z>0)$ is given by

$$H=\frac{1}{\sqrt{(1-z^2)(1-k^2z^2)}}$$ (X1-3)

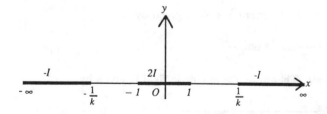

Fig. X1-2 (b) Parallel thin plates

Therefore, the inductance per unit length is given by

$$L=\mu\left|\frac{\displaystyle\int_{3'}Hdz}{2\displaystyle\int_{-43}Hdz}\right|=\mu\frac{K(k')}{4K(k)} \qquad\text{(X1-3)}$$

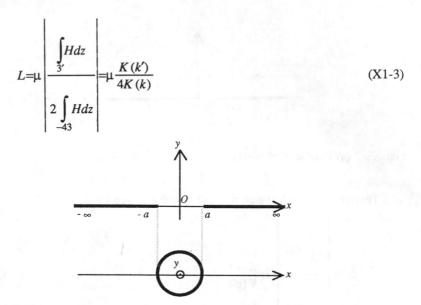

Fig. X1-3 Thin annulus

The scalar potential Φ of Fig. X1-3 has only ξ component, where

$$x=a\cosh\xi\cos\eta\cos\phi \qquad\text{(X1-4-1)}$$

$$y=a\cosh\xi\cos\eta\sin\phi \qquad\text{(X1-4-2)}$$

$$z=a\sinh\xi\sin\eta, \qquad\text{(X1-4-3)}$$

When the total current is 1, Φ is given by

$$\Phi=-\frac{1}{\pi}\tan^{-1}\sinh\xi+\frac{1}{2} \qquad\text{(X1-5)}$$

because $\Delta\Phi=0$. Therefore, the magnetic field is given by

$$H=\frac{1}{\pi a\cosh\xi\sqrt{\sinh^2\xi+\sin^2\eta}} \qquad\text{(X1-6)}$$

When $\xi=0$ (on the hole),

$$H=\frac{1}{\pi\sqrt{a^2-r^2}}, \qquad\text{(X1-6-1)}$$

where $r=a\cos\eta$. The inductance is the flux of the hole and is given by

$$L=\mu\int_0^a \frac{2\pi r}{\pi\sqrt{a^2-r^2}}dr=2a\mu \qquad\qquad\text{(X1-7)}$$

QFP QFP Logic (QQL) [†]

Willy Hioe[*], Mutsumi Hosoya[*] and Eiichi Goto[*** * **]

Abstract

The correct operation of a Quantum Flux Parametron is affected by a number of internal and external problems. Among internal problems are the variation of Josephson junction critical currents, the flux loss in transformer self-inductances and variations in transformer coupling. External problems are caused by interaction between QFPs in the same network and include relay noise, homophase noise and reaction hazard. QFP logic circuits have so far been based on wired-majority logic which being a linear input logic has an inherently low margin. This paper describes three circuits for solving the internal problems. A booster deals with the problem of imbalance between the critical currents of Josephson junctions in a QFP while a regulator ensures full activation of QFPs. A puller increases the activation input impedance and reduces flux loss in activation inductors. Lastly, a non-threshold gate is proposed which solves or reduces the external problems as well as increases the input margin. This new gate gives birth to a new QFP logic family which we call QQL (for QFP QFP Logic).

1.Introduction

The Quantum Flux Parametron (QFP) [1, 2] is a unique superconducting flux-based Josephson device. Using QFPs, it is possible to build a computer whose logic elements work completely on the storage and transmission of flux. Theoretical analysis shows that it has a power dissipation in the order of 1nW at 10-GHz clock [2, 3].

Designs of logic circuits using QFPs have until now only considered the use of QFPs as flux amplifiers [4, 5, 6]. Logic functions are produced with wired-logic, adding either currents or fluxes. Since wired-logic is a form of linear input logic, these logic circuits have inherently low margins. A QFP's correct operation may

---

[†] Revised

[*] Research Development Corporation of Japan (JRDC), Goto Quantum Magneto-Flux Logic Project, c/o Hitachi Central Research Laboratory, 1-280, Higashi-Koigakubo, Kokubunji, Tokyo 185, Japan, Tel. 0423-25-7881, Fax. 0424-25-1783

[**] The Institute of Physical and Chemical Research (RIKEN), 2-1 Hirosawa, Wako-shi, Saitama 351-01, Japan.

[***] University of Tokyo, Faculty of Science, Department of Information Science, 7-3-1 Hongo, Bunkyo-ku, Tokyo, Japan.

also be affected if the pair of Josephson junctions it contains have unequal critical supercurrents or if it interacts adversely with other elements in a circuit. These problems make the design of large QFP circuits a formidable task.

QFPs are suitable for building 3-dimensional circuits [7] because the flux output enables magnetically coupled connections between circuits on two chips stacked together. When the activation or clock signal of QFPs is also applied across the gap between two chips, the effective activation flux may vary between QFPs because of an uneven gap so that some QFPs may not be fully activated.

This paper describes three circuits which overcome or alleviate the above problems. A novel non-threshold logic gate is also proposed which uses QFPs for the logic operation and greatly reduces interaction between gates, resulting in much improved margin. It is possible to build all logic functions using only gates of this type. A number of useful logic operations in fact require only one gate.

In the following 2 sections, the operation of the basic QFP is first described followed by a brief look at wired-majority QFP logic. Next the problems faced by the basic QFP and wired-majority logic is discussed. The three circuits for dealing with these problems are examined in sections 4 to 6. The non-threshold gate is introduced in section 7 and example uses of this gate are given in section 8. Finally section 9 summarizes the main results presented in this paper.

2. The Quantum Flux Parametron

A QFP consists of a pair of Josephson junctions connected in series and a pair of transformers which are used to apply equal and opposite phase angle biases to the Josephson junction pair. An input line and an output inductor are connected to the midpoint between the junctions. Fig. 1 illustrates the basic QFP scheme.

The quasi-static characteristics of the QFP may be analyzed from its Hamiltonian which expressed in dimensionless units is given, except for a constant term, by

$$u = \frac{1}{2}b\left(\phi - \beta\right)^2 - \cos\phi\cos\alpha \tag{1}$$

The first term on the right is the potential energy of the load and the second is that of the Josephson junction pair. ϕ is the magnetic flux across the load inductor expressed in generalized flux angle which is defined as

$$\phi = \frac{\Phi}{\Phi_0} 2\pi \qquad (2)$$

where $\Phi_0 = h/2e$ is the unit quantum flux. α is the activation flux angle. β is the input current expressed as a flux angular bias to the load. b is the inductance factor of the load, and may also be referred to as the load factor. If L is the load inductance, I_J is the critical current of each Josephson junction and $I_Q = 2I_J$ then b is defined by

$$b = \frac{\Phi_0}{2\pi I_Q L} \qquad (3)$$

The stable states are given by solving for ϕ in

$$\frac{du}{d\phi} = b\left(\phi - \beta\right) + \sin \phi \cos \alpha = 0 \qquad (4)$$

$$\frac{d^2u}{d\phi^2} = b + \cos \phi \cos \alpha > 0 \qquad (5)$$

It may be noticed that equation (4) expresses the current relationship in dimensionless terms and is none other than Kirchhoff's current equation. This equation by itself is insufficient to determine the stable states of the circuit since there is no corresponding voltage equation and equation (5) is needed.

In Graph 1, the QFP activation characteristics is shown for $\alpha=0$ to 180 degrees but it is also true for α which differs by an integer multiple of 2π rads. The discussion below assumes the general case. The input flux angle, β, is assumed to be positive for ease of explanation. For negative inputs, the graph is a reflection over the α axis. As $\cos\alpha$ varies from 1 to -1, at first the output flux angle, ϕ, is less than β. When $\cos \alpha = 0$, $\phi=\beta$. Thereafter, ϕ increases rapidly, reaching a maximum when $\cos \alpha = -1$. At this activation level, if the load factor b is less than 1, then even if the input signal is removed the output flux angle does not drop to zero. The output drops to zero only by changing the activation signal so that $\cos \alpha$ becomes sufficiently large again or by changing the load so that b becomes greater than 1. Hence, the QFP has the ability to store a signal, that is, it has a memory effect. When b is less than 1, we can say the QFP is operating in the memory mode.

If b is greater than or equal to 1, then as soon as the input signal is removed, the output flux of the activated QFP drops to zero. There is no memory effect. The QFP behaves only as a flux amplifier, and we can say it is operating in the amplifying mode. It should be noted that the output signal level depends on the input signal level. The memory mode is the normal mode of QFP operation. Hereafter, unless specifically stated otherwise, all QFPs may be assumed to be operating in this mode.

The amplification effect of a QFP may be understood by considering only the combined energy of the Josephson junctions. When $\cos \alpha = 1$, an energy minimum exists for $\phi = 0$. But as activation level increases and $\cos \alpha$ becomes gradually smaller, an energy maximum appears at $\phi = 0$. This is an unstable equilibrium state and any disturbance, no matter how small, will cause the equilibrium to move to an energy minimum state. Thus, it may be seen that a small input can cause a relatively large change to ϕ. The effect is graphically illustrated in Fig. 2. In an ideal case where no noise disturbs the equilibrium, the amplification is infinitely large. However, in practical operation the amplification is very much reduced by noise. Also, because of noise the input must be applied before activation starts.

The two energy minima next to the abovementioned energy maximum, one for positive ϕ and the other for negative ϕ are the two possible activated states for normal operation. Hence the QFP is a bistable device. Positive and negative fluxes represent the binary values.

Before the energy maximum appears, only one Josephson junction supplies current to the load. But after the energy maximum appears, the current in one Josephson junction changes direction and both Josephson junctions now supply current to the load. Since the Josephson junction's supercurrent is largest when the phase angle across the junction is $\pm\pi/2$, maximum load current of twice the Josephson junctions' critical current is obtained when both junctions supply current to the load, the output flux angle is $\pm\pi/2$, and the activation flux angle is $\pm\pi$.

3. QFP Logic Circuits

We will now look at how QFPs can be used in wired-logic circuits. The simplest example of a wired-logic "device" is the junction of a number of input wires and an output wire. The output is the algebraic sum of the inputs. It is clear that if logic value '0' is represented by no signal and '1' by any positive signal then the above junction performs an OR function correctly. With QFPs, if the input signals have equal absolute values and an odd number of them exist then the junction performs a MAJORITY function. The basic circuit is shown in Fig. 4. Since the output signal level depends on the majority margin it must be restored to the correct level after a logical operation. A QFP is used for this purpose as well as to provide sufficient fan-out.

Used in the memory mode, an activated QFP holds a signal well and its state cannot be easily changed by normal input signal levels. QFPs have to be specifically quenched to remove the stored signals. Hence, each QFP in a circuit goes through a cycle of activation and quenching. Logic signals are transmitted through a network by a process of baton-passing. QFPs providing the input signals to a wired-OR junction and that restoring the signal level of the output (probably also providing input to the next wired-majority junction) are activated by signals which differ in phase. These activation signals are referred to as subclocks. A minimum of three subclocks are needed. Because QFPs are two-terminal devices, output signals from active QFPs flow backwards into the input circuitry. If two subclocks are used, the direction of signal flow is indeterminate and input signals are corrupted by signals from the output side.

4. Problems faced by QFPs

A variety of problems may affect the optimum performance of QFPs, which are,

internal causes

- δI noise
- transformer inductance
- transformer coupling

external causes

- relay noise
- homophase noise

138

- reaction hazard

- input level fluctuation

δI Noise

It is clear that a QFP provides optimum amplification only if the Josephson junctions and activation fluxes are perfectly matched. Only a very small input signal is needed to determine the output which in the ideal case is infinitely large. In practice, it is difficult to fabricate Josephson junctions precisely and a fairly large variation in the critical current is obtained even between Josephson junctions made on the same chip. As a result, the critical currents of the two Josephson junctions in the QFP are not balanced causing wrong output polarity. This problem is known as δI noise.

We can qualitatively understand the problem by considering the Josephson junctions' combined energy again. When the critical currents are not balanced, the energy maximum we saw before does not occur at $\phi=0$ when $\cos \alpha \neq -1$. An effective bias appears. As a result, for a small input signal the imbalance may cause the output to go into the wrong energy minimum as shown in Fig. 6.

The minimum input strength that gives correct output, ignoring other noise problems, can be found as follows. It is clear that the output flux angle when the local maximum first appears should be greater in absolute value than the local maximum's deviation from $\phi = 0$. At the limit, the deviation is equal to the output flux angle. Considering the energy-ϕ curve, the limiting condition is that the QFP state is at the local maximum when it first appears. Since the local maximum appears together with a new local minimum, that is, at an inflexion point, then together with the original energy minimum these turning points of the ϕ-energy curve are triple roots of the equation

$$\frac{du}{d\phi} = 0 \tag{6}$$

where

$$u = \frac{1}{2}b\left(\phi - \beta\right)^2 - \cos \phi \cos \alpha \pm \delta I \sin \phi \sin \alpha \tag{7}$$

In other words, it must also be true that

$$\frac{d^2u}{d\phi^2} = 0 \quad , \qquad \frac{d^3u}{d\phi^3} = 0 \tag{8}$$

The solution to equations (6) and (8) is plotted in Graph 2. The minimum input angle depends both on the load factor b and δI. For the same load, a larger δI requires an almost proportionally larger input for correct operation.

Transformer Inductance

In equation (1), it was assumed that transformers used to provide activation fluxes do not contribute to the total energy. In practice, transformers have finite leakage and shunting inductances. If these inductances are large significant energy quantities may be stored in them. As a result the effective activation flux angles across the Josephson junctions may be significantly reduced so that more activation flux has to be applied before the QFP switches. However, when the current in one junction switches direction, the flux from the transformer self inductance has a positive effect and the effective activation flux angle increases rapidly. The effect of transformer inductance on the activation characteristics may be found from the energy as before.

$$u = \frac{1}{2}b\left(\phi - \beta\right)^2 + \frac{1}{2}a\left(\alpha - \theta\right)^2 - \cos\phi\cos\theta \tag{9}$$

The new symbols are: θ, the effective activation flux angle and a, the inductance factor of the transformer self-inductance. In equation (9), the second term on the right is for the energy stored in the transformer's self-inductance. The relation between ϕ and α are found from

$$\frac{\partial u}{\partial \phi} = 0, \frac{\partial u}{\partial \theta} = 0 \tag{10}$$

such that the Hesse matrix

$$H_2(u) = \begin{vmatrix} \dfrac{\partial^2 u}{\partial \phi^2} & \dfrac{\partial^2 u}{\partial \phi\, \partial \theta} \\ \dfrac{\partial^2 u}{\partial \theta\, \partial \phi} & \dfrac{\partial^2 u}{\partial \theta^2} \end{vmatrix} \tag{11}$$

is positive definite. The result is plotted in Graph 3. It may be noted that for large transformer inductances, a hysteresis appears in the activation characteristics. The activation and de-activation paths are different.

Using small activation transformer inductances result in a different set of problems. A large activation current, as much as 10 times the QFP output current, will be necessary. Crosstalk between activation and signal lines is a major problem. It may also be noted that the output from a single QFP will be insufficient for activating another similar QFP.

Transformer Coupling

In the introduction, it has been noted that the QFP is suitable for building 3-dimensional circuits. Details of the proposed structure are in a separate paper [12]. For our purpose, it is only necessary to note that gates without the activation lines are made on a chip, and activation lines together with wiring between gates will be on another chip. The magnetic coupling at different parts of the chip surface may vary because of uneven gap between chips. A weak coupling will lead to weaker logic signals and inadequate activation. Similar problems occur in the case of monolithic circuits but to a lesser degree, for example, due to mask misalignment in the fabrication process. The output strength at various levels of activation may be seen from Graph 4. When the activation varies from the optimum by more than 30% the output falls drastically.

Relay Noise

The QFP is a two-terminal device, that is, its input and output share the same port. There is no direction built into the device and amplified signals may flow backwards into the input circuitry. Transistors, in comparison, are 3-terminal devices with separate input and output ports. The bilateral property of QFPs leads to two problems: reduced fan-out and relay noise.

A de-activated or quenched QFP has a low output impedance so sizeable backcurrent can flow from QFPs in the next stage through lines connecting them. The forward current from an active QFP is reduced by the amount flowing backwards into the input circuitry and hence, the fan-out is reduced. With a large fan-in, an additional QFP stage may be needed to give sufficient fan-out.

The more critical problem is relay noise. The backcurrent is partly shunted to ground by the quenched QFPs it passes through. The proportion shunted depends on the ratio between a quenched QFP's equivalent inductance and the total inductance of circuitry further back as seen from this QFP. The balance is coupled or "relayed" backwards. When these signals are relayed to a QFP about to be activated they compete with the true input signals for control of the QFP output. Because the noise comes through intervening quenched QFPs it is called Relay Noise.

Relay noise can be reduced by increasing the number of subclocks because each quenched QFP on the relay noise path acts as a shunt and reduces the noise level. More subclocks means more quenched stages between two active stages. For example, if the relay factor of a quenched QFP is 0.2, that is, 20% of the backcurrent passes through, then the combined relay factor of two quenched stages is 0.04 or 5 times less.

Relay noise is also reduced if more backcurrent is shunted to ground. This can be achieved by increasing the inductance of input/output lines relative to the shunt inductance which happens to be the equivalent inductance of a quenched QFP. However, a larger input/output line inductance means smaller input signals which may not be possible because of the δI noise and other noise problems. It can be seen that solution of the δI noise problem will help to reduce the relay noise problem.

Homophase Noise

When QFPs in the same activation stage do not switch together but some switch earlier than others, the output current from QFPs switched earlier may affect the input to QFPs switched later. Since the problem occurs between QFPs in the same phase, it is known as *Homophase Noise*. Three causes for homophase noise may be identified: clock skew which is the delay between clock signals, activation delay due to activation transformer inductances, and variation in activation transformer coupling. Two types of homophase noise exist: relayed and direct.

Relayed homophase noise occurs when the output current from an active QFP is relayed backwards at a wired-majority junction as shown in Fig. 8. The worst effect is on the last QFP to be activated. Unlike relay noise, relayed homophase noise cannot be reduced by increasing the number of activation phases since the number of quenched QFPs on the relay path is exactly one.

Direct homophase noise happens in the case of cascaded QFPs as shown in Fig. 9. The output current from active QFPs flow directly to the unswitched QFPs. There are no intermediate quenched QFPs to absorb part of the noise current. The effect on a QFP about to be activated can be much larger than normal input signals and the danger of a wrong output is greater than in the case of relayed homophase noise.

Clock skew can be reduced by activating QFPs in the same phase on the same activation lines. The activation line inductance of an active QFP is larger than that for a quenched QFP. Hence, the activation of a QFP has the effect of increasing the activation current to other QFPs on the same activation line. Each activation increases the activation current further. Thus, an avalanche effect is achieved and delay between activations is reduced.

Reaction Hazard

Homophase noise concerns the effect of active QFPs on other inactive QFPs that are activated in the same stage. Reaction hazard concerns the effect of active QFPs on one another. The state of an active QFP, although very stable, can be changed if driven by sufficiently strong currents.

Reaction hazard may cause the output polarity to reverse if the reaction current and the output current flow in opposite directions. On the other hand, if the reaction current is in the same direction, higher mode error may occur, that is, the output is shifted higher by about 2π radians in flux angle. Even if polarity reversal or higher mode error do not occur the fluctuations of the output current is one of the causes of the next problem.

Input Signal Fluctuation

The signal strengths of the inputs to the wired-majority gate discussed above may vary because of variations in the Josephson junction critical currents, variations in the activation levels, variations in the load inductance, and other noises. When the minority inputs have almost equal combined signal strength than that of the majority inputs, the algebraic sum of the inputs may be below the minimum input signal strength for the output QFP. A wrong output may result. If the combined minority input strength is greater the output will be determined by the minority inputs. This problem is intrinsic to linear input logics [cf. 8] such as the wired-majority gates discussed so far. In the 3-input majority gate shown in Fig. 11, the inputs cannot vary by more than ±33% from their design values. The margin decreases with the fan-in.

Each of the above problems, by itself, may have a serious effect on the correct operation of QFP circuits. Together, they severely reduce the device margin and present a formidable problem to the circuit designer. The circuits proposed in this paper, which we will now see, are designed to solve or at least alleviate all the problems mentioned so far.

5. Booster

A booster alleviates the δI noise problem. It is actually a pre-activated basic QFP connected in series with another basic QFP. The scheme for a QFP with booster is shown in Fig. 12.

The booster is activated either by direct current or by a split activation method and does not require another subclock. δI noise is small in a booster because of the following reason. The normalized potential energy in the booster's Josephson junction pair is given by

$$u_{jj} = -\cos \alpha \cos \phi \pm \delta I \sin \alpha \sin \phi \qquad (12)$$

At full activation, if the activation flux varies from $\alpha = \pm \pi$ by $\delta \pi$, then the change in u_{jj}, δu_{jj}, is given approximately by

$$\delta u_{jj} = \pm \delta I \, \delta \pi \sin \phi \qquad (13)$$

Since δu_{jj} is proportional to the product of δI and $\delta \pi$, it is a second order variation. By fully activating the booster during the QFP's transitional state, the effect from its δI noise is almost completely absent and only the QFP's δI noise needs to be dealt with.

The δI noise characteristics of a boostered-QFP is found as in the case of the basic QFP. The energy is given by

$$u = \frac{1}{2}b\left(\phi - \beta\right)^2 - \cos\phi\cos\alpha + \cos\phi \pm \delta I \sin\phi\sin\alpha \qquad (14)$$

The triple root is found from similar equations

$$\frac{du}{d\phi} = 0, \ \frac{d^2u}{d\phi^2} = 0, \ \frac{d^3u}{d\phi^3} = 0 \qquad (15)$$

and Graph 5 shows the results.

The load factor in the graph is for a single QFP so in the case of a boostered-QFP which produces twice as much current, the corresponding load factor which gives the same output flux angle is twice as large. Comparing Graph 2 and Graph 5 , the minimum input for a given critical current imbalance is almost the same as that for a single QFP. However, since maximum output current is doubled the gain is significantly better. When the load is chosen to provide maximum output current, the maximum gain when δI noise = ±10% is almost 22 times. Some of the additional gain can be traded for a larger margin.

A disadvantage of a booster is its amplification of relay noise if it is always active. When the booster is activated and the QFP is quenched, relay noise is not quenched by the QFP because the booster amplifies the relay noise by an amount exactly equal to that shunted by the quenched QFP. The quenched QFP's shunting effect is cancelled and relay noise is fully transmitted. The problem can be solved if the booster is activated at the same time as the QFP or immediately before. In the former case, its activation has to reach full level before the QFP switches. We will show one way how this can be done in the next section.

6. Puller

In the scheme shown in Fig. 13 a puller is a pair of Josephson junctions sharing the QFP's activation lines. Its input is constantly at $\pm\pi$. Its effect on the activation line is in some ways similar to that of a booster on the input line, that is, it increases the impedance of the activation line. Like the booster it is pre-activated so that it operates like a current source. The pulled QFP's characteristics is shown in Graph 6.

inductors and the Josephson junction so that only half of the unshunted flux angle is obtained. The regulator output flux angle is zero. If the input flux angle is close to π, the Josephson current flows in the opposite direction and increases the shunt flux angle. The additional flux angle is almost proportional to twice the difference of α from π so that the regulator output is nearly π. The output jumps from nearly zero to nearly π when the Josephson current switches directions.

When a load is connected, the load current draws flux from the transformers so that it appears as if a smaller input flux is applied. The regulator input-output characteristics curve (for positive α) is shifted towards π.

If the flux drawn by the load is small compared to the regulator input flux then the delay it causes to the regulator output is small. The delay can be reduced if the number of unshunted parallel inductors in the regulator is increased. The effect is to reduce the flux loss per inductor in these unshunted inductors so that a larger flux angle is applied to the Josephson junction without proportionately losing more flux to the load. Hence, the Josephson junction shunt is made to switch at a smaller output flux angle.

8. D-Gate: a Non-Linear-Input QFP Logic Gate

The QFP can be used as a logic element by itself instead of only as an amplifier such as in the wired-majority logic described before. If the activation clock signal is replaced by the output of one or more QFPs, the output of a QFP activated in this way becomes a function of two or more inputs. A QFP activated by the output of other QFPs will be known as a Variable Activation QFP or VAQ.

Let us consider how the activation flux is produced. A QFP's output varies with its load as shown in Graph 8. For large and small load inductances, the output current is small. Maximum current equal to the combined current of the Josephson junctions is obtained when the load factor is $2/\pi$ or when the output flux angle is $\pi/2$. In terms of flux angle, the output is π for zero load factor, monotonically decreases with increase in load factor, and is zero for load factors greater than one. Because of the low current output, larger higher mode hazard and large inductance, an output flux angle near π is not preferred. In the D-gate which is described below, two driving QFPs are used to activate a VAQ. Each produce a flux angle of

$\pi/2$, hence they are designed to produce maximum current.

By adding the output flux of two driving QFPs $\pm\pi$ is obtained which is also the activation flux angle for fully activating a QFP. If the inputs of the driving QFPs are s and t, and the VAQ's input is x then the VAQ's output logic function is

$$x\left(st + \overline{s}\overline{t}\right) \tag{21}$$

However, this is true only when s and t have the same polarity. When they have opposite polarities, the VAQ's activation flux angle is zero, the VAQ is not activated and the VAQ's input is not amplified. Nevertheless, there is a small output with the same polarity as x since the VAQ is a 2-terminal device. Thus, a VAQ, by itself would function as a 3-state logic gate.

In the D-Gate, a pair of VAQs are activated by the same driving QFPs. One VAQ will be activated by the sum and the other by the difference of the driving QFP outputs. The VAQ output fluxes are added to give the D-Gate's output. Assuming that x and y are the inputs, and s and t are the driving QFP inputs, the D-Gate performs the logic function

$$x\left(st + \overline{s}\overline{t}\right) + y\left(\overline{s}t + s\overline{t}\right) \tag{22}$$

This logic function is always true and the D-Gate operates as a 2-state logic gate.

The basic scheme of the D-Gate is shown in Fig. 16. Each VAQ is a QFP with a puller because, as explained earlier, a QFP's output is too small to drive a QFP without a puller. Boosters are attached to the driving QFPs as well as the VAQs to overcome δI noise. The driving QFPs are activated by clock signals. To ensure full activation, the activation transformers are fitted with regulators. Boosters are preactivated by attaching pullers to their activation lines.

Let us consider the properties of the D-Gate with respect to the interaction noise problems found in wired-majority logic. It has a smaller relay noise problem. Any backcurrent is first partially shunted by a quenched booster. The balance is further shunted by the inactive VAQs. Compared to the basic QFP a smaller relay factor is obtained. On the other hand, the use of booster allows a larger fan-out. Thus, when the fan-out is large, some additional scheme to reduce relay noise may be necessary, for example, using a negative feedback to cancel relay noise. The relay noise through the VAQ activation lines is negligible because the quenched driving QFPs are very effective shunts.

Homophase noise is negligible. There is no direct homophase noise between the VAQs in a D-Gate since only one will be activated at any one time. In the case of the driving QFPs, the reverse coupling in the activation transformer and the VAQ's high activation impedance effectively separate their outputs. Relayed homophase noise between D-Gates is small as input lines are not directly connected in a network using only D-gates. Some current may be relayed through the connection between VAQ outputs in a D-Gate. However, since there are 2 VAQs in the relay path, most of the homophase noise current will be shunted. Examples of relay noise and homophase noise for the D-gate are illustrated in Figs. 17 and 18.

Reaction hazard for the same reason as homophase noise will be negligible.

The input margin for the D-Gate is much improved. The fan-in for each component device (VAQ or driving QFP) in the D-Gate is one but since VAQs are two terminal devices and their outputs are connected, their inputs interact to some degree with each other. The interaction is small because the output impedance of the VAQ that is activated becomes very large whereas the inactive VAQ's output impedance remains small. The ratio is 6 times or more. Hence, the inactive VAQ has a very small output and the interaction is negligible. This also means that the VAQ inputs can differ by a ratio of 6 or more times. Fig. 19 illustrates how the inputs interact via the VAQ output connection.

9. QQL

The way that a D-Gate uses the QFP in the form of a VAQ to perform logic functions is analogous to TTL where logic functions are performed within transistors. Historically, both are first used as amplification devices. Hence, if the "T" in TTL is replaced by the "Q" of QFP, what is obtained is QQL. The D-Gate has given birth to a new QFP logic family which is analogous to the TTL logic family in transistor technology.

Taking the analogy further, wired-majority QFP logic may be seen as Inductor QFP Logic or IQL which is analogous to RTL (Resistor Transistor Logic). In fact, like IQL, RTL is a kind of threshold logic. The inductor in IQL serves a similar function to the resistor in RTL. In the history of transistors, RTL was followed by DTL (Diode Transistor Logic). The equivalent of DTL would exist if Josephson junctions are used as circuit elements. Since a Josephson junction does not pass current when the phase angle across it is an integer multiple of π, it has diode-like properties although the margin is very small. In fact, a parity circuit which uses the Josephson junction in place of the load inductor has been proposed by Osawa [6]. The history of QQL seems to have paralleled that of transistors at least up to TTL.

The analogy, however, does not extend to QQL logic functions. Whereas TTL is a NAND gate which is in the family of invertor-type gates, the D-Gate is a multiplexor or a kind of relay switch which places it in the family of relay logics. However, because parametron-type logic devices are bistable in non-zero states instead of a zero state and a non-zero state such as in transistor logic devices, their use as switches differs from classical switching circuits. The former is a non-zero switch while the latter is a zero switch.

Consider the typical zero-type relay circuit in Fig. 20. The output f is an AND function of the input, a, and the control signal, b. If the low signal is logical '0', the non-detection of a signal at f is interpreted as a '0' signal. Thus, sending a '0' signal means not sending any signal at all. More correctly, the output is allowed to float. This is a cause of wrong operation and usually relay logic circuits are designed so that outputs do not float. In each relay circuit, at least one relay path must go through. This design principle leads to complementary or differential combinational circuits as shown in Fig. 21.

In the case of non-zero switching circuits, a default signal, not necessarily the '0' signal, must actually be sent. Fig. 22 illustrates the idea. One of the selectable inputs must be the default signal, '0' in this case. If '1' is the default and c is set to '0' then the circuit implements a 2-input NAND function.

Setting one input to a default signal does not realize the full power of D-Gates. It is a complementary switch and complementary relay circuits are more appropriate.

A general method based on the well-known Shannon expansion theorem [9, 10] exists for generating complementary relay circuits. A logic function can be systematically reduced to functions with fewer variables using equation (23).

$$f(x_1, x_2, \cdots, x_n) = x_1 f(1, x_2, \cdots, x_n) + \overline{x_1} f(0, x_2, \cdots, x_n) \qquad (23)$$

Repeated applications of the theorem rapidly reduces the original function to single variables. It is clear that exactly one of the two smaller expressions will be selected. Thus, there will be exactly one through path in the synthesized circuit.

Using the Shannon expansion theorem may not lead to the minimum circuit because the select signal is a single variable whereas in the D-Gate it is a function of two variables. Let us look at a number of important logical functions with 4 or fewer variables which use only one D-Gate. For example, the majority and parity functions used by a full adder require only one D-gate each. If the D-Gate's output function is

$$D(s, t; x, y) = x\left(st + \bar{s}\bar{t}\right) + y\left(\bar{s}t + s\bar{t}\right) \tag{24}$$

then the 3-input Majority and 3-input Parity functions are

$$M(x, y, z) = xy + yz + zx = D(x, y ; x, z) \tag{25}$$

$$P(x, y, z) = xyz + x\bar{y}\bar{z} + \bar{x}y\bar{z} + \bar{x}\bar{y}z = D(x, y ; z, \bar{z}) \tag{26}$$

In fact, if we note that the select signals of the majority and parity functions are the same, it may be seen that they can be combined and a full adder gate can be build with only 2 driving QFPs. Examples of the majority, parity and full adder gates are shown in Figs. 23 to 25.

The latching effect of the D-gate makes it suitable for pipeline designs. For example, a multiplier can be built using 2-bit AND gates, full adders and majority gates each of which requires only one level of D-Gates. Partial products are first obtained using 2-bit AND gates. A Wallace tree of full adders reduce the partial products to two bit-vectors which are added using carry lookahead addition. An XY-symmetric carry lookahead adder [cf. 11] can be built from majority gates. Instead of a generate bit and a propagate bit the block carry status of bit positions i through j is encoded in two bits in the following way:

$$X(i,j) = Y(i,j) = H \qquad \text{Generate}$$

$$X(i,j) <> Y(i,j) \qquad \text{Propagate}$$

$$X(i,j) = Y(i,j) = L \qquad \text{No Carry}$$

Hence,

$$G(i,j) = X(i,j)\, Y(i,j)$$

$$P(i,j) = X(i,j) \neq Y(i,j)$$

Each XY-block takes four operands and generates two outputs as follows:

$$X = x_1 . (x_1 = y_1) + x_0 . (x_1 \neq y_1)$$
$$= M(x_0, x_1, y_1)$$
$$Y = y_1 . (x_1 = y_1) + y_0 . (x_1 \neq y_1)$$
$$= M(y_0, x_1, y_1)$$

Fig. 26 shows the gates in an XY-block and Fig. 27 shows two stages of XY-blocks. A minimal 4x4 multiplier is shown without the 2-bit AND gates in Fig. 28. Since the multiplier is fully pipelined its clock rate is equal to that of the D-Gate.

The D-Gate has been tested at 10GHz by computer simulation using SPICE with the following parameters:

$I_J = 50\ \mu A$	: JJ characteristic current	
$R_J = 350\Omega$	: JJ normal resistance	
$C_J = 0.5\ pF$	: JJ capacitance	
$R_S = 4\ \Omega$	: JJ shunt resistance	
$L_{IO} = 20pH$	: I/O transformer inductances	
$L_P = 2\ pH$	: Puller activation inductance	
$L_R = 1.5\ pH$	: Regulator inductance	
$I_R = 100\ \mu A$	: Regulator shunt JJ characteristic current	
$L_D = 5\ pH$	: Load inductance	

The transient response is shown in Plot 1. This shows that the quasi-static analysis which is based on stable states gives a sufficiently accurate description of the D-Gate operation.

10. Summary

Three circuits, a booster, a puller and a regulator have been described in this paper which separately improves the characteristics of the QFP against internal problems. In the case of the booster, the QFP's vulnerability to relay noise is also alleviated. The puller enables the design of the D-Gate, a non-threshold logic gate which is much stronger against the external problems of wired-majority QFP logic.

Moreover, with the D-Gate 3-input majority and parity functions can be implemented in one gate. It was shown that with this possibility, together with the latching property of D-Gates, a fully pipelined multiplier operating at the D-Gate clock frequency can be built. Finally, SPICE simulation results of the D-gate was presented.

Acknowledgements

The authors wish to thank the Science and Technology Agency of Japan which sponsored the ERATO project under which this research was done. We also thank the Hitachi Central Research Laboratory for using their computer to do our SPICE simulations. The static characteristics given in this paper are obtained from programs written in MATHEMATICA™*, a computer package for symbolic and numerical mathematical calculations. (An equivalent FORTRAN program for computing the characteristics of a QFP with puller is given in appendix A.)

References

1. Goto, E., "Josephson Pair Elements", *Proc. of the 1st RIKEN Symposium on Josephson Electronics*, 1984, pp48-51, (in Japanese).
2. Goto, E. & Loe, K.F., *DC Flux Parametron*: World Scientific, Singapore, 1986.
3. Harada, Y., Nakane, H., Miyamoto, N., Kawabe, U., Goto, E. & Soma, T., "Basic Operations of the Quantum Flux Parametron", *IEEE Trans. Magnetics*, vol MAG-23, No. 5, Sep 1987, pp3801-3807.
4. Harada, Y., Miyamoto, N. & Goto, E., "Experimental Results on QFP", *Proc. of 3rd RIKEN Symposium on Josephson Electronics*, Mar 1986, pp53-58 (in Japanese).
5. Harada, Y. & Goto, E., "Experimental Results on QFP", *Proc. of 4th RIKEN Symposium on Josephson Electronics*, Mar 1987, pp68-74 (in Japanese).
6. Osawa, N., "A Study of Inductive Josephson Logic" in *Fluxoid Josephson Computer Technology*, (ed) Goto, E., Soma, T. & Loe, K.F.: World

---

*   *Mathematica* is a trademark of Wolfram Research, Inc.

Scientific, Singapore, 1988

7. Harada, Y., Hosoya, M., Goto, E. & Kamikawai, R., "A Study on the QFP Packaging System", *Proc. of 6th RIKEN Symposium on Josephson Electronics*, Mar 1989, pp54-70 (in Japanese).

8. Lewis, P.M. & Coates, C.L., *Threshold Logic*: John Wiley, 1967.

9. Shannon, C.E., "A Symbolic Analysis of Relay and Switching Circuits", in *Trans. AIEE*, Vol 57, 1938, pp713-723.

10. Shannon, C.E., "The Synthesis of Two-terminal Switching Circuits", *Bell Syst. Tech. J.*, Vol 28, No 1, 1949.

11. Takahashi, H., (ed) *Parametron Computer*: Iwanami, Japan 1969. (In Japanese)

12. Kamikawai, R., Harada, Y., Hosoya, M., Hioe, W., Wada, Y., Nakane, H. & Goto, E., "Basic Technology for Three-Dimensional Packages," presented at 7th RIKEN Symposium (this meeting).

Appendix A

An example of the analysis to obtain static characteristics of a QFP circuit is given.

The puller described in section 5 is considered. The normalized energy is given by

$$u = \frac{1}{2}b\left(\phi - \beta\right)^2 - \cos\phi\cos\theta + \cos\theta + \frac{1}{2}a\left(\alpha - \theta\right)^2 \qquad \text{(A.1)}$$

The equilibrium points are given by

$$\frac{\partial u}{\partial \phi} = b\left(\phi - \beta\right) + \sin\phi\cos\theta = 0 \qquad \text{(A.2)}$$

$$\frac{\partial u}{\partial \theta} = \cos\phi\sin\theta - \sin\theta - a\left(\alpha - \theta\right) = 0 \qquad \text{(A.3)}$$

From equation (A.2), θ can be found in terms of ϕ,

$$\theta = \cos^{-1}\left(\frac{-b\left(\phi - \beta\right)}{\sin\phi}\right) \qquad \text{(A.4)}$$

Substituting this in equation (A.3), α can be found in terms of ϕ.

$$\alpha = \frac{\left(\cos\phi\sin\theta - \sin\theta\right)}{a} + \theta \qquad \text{(A.5)}$$

In the general case, the variables cannot be separated and finding a solution to simultaneous non-linear equations will be necessary.

A Fortran program to generate data points for the puller characteristics graph is given below.

```
IMPLICIT REAL (P)
DATA PI/3.14159/
DO 20 I=1,5
  A=0.2*I
CALL PULLER(A,2.0/PI,22.5,0,180,5)
  WRITE(6,*) ' '
```

```fortran
   20 CONTINUE
      STOP
      END
      SUBROUTINE PULLER(A,B,BTDEG,I1,I2,I3)
      DATA PI/3.14159/
      WRITE(6,*) 'Split Activation of Push Pull QFPs'
      WRITE(6,*) '  A        B        BTDEG        I1        I2        I3'
      WRITE(6,100) A,B,BTDEG,I1,I2,I3
  100 FORMAT(1H ,3F8.3,3I8)
      WRITE(6,*) 'AlphaDEG ThetaDEG FiDEG'
      BT=BTDEG*PI/180.0
      DO 10 I=I1,I2,I3
        FDEG=I*1.0
        F=I*PI/180.0
        IF (F.EQ.0.0) THEN
          CT=1.0
        ELSE
          CT=-B*(F-BT)/SIN(F)
        ENDIF
        IF (CT.LT.0.0) THEN
          ABSCT = -CT
        ELSE
          ABSCT = CT
        ENDIF
        IF (ABSCT.LE.1.0) THEN
          T=ACOS(CT)
          AL=T+SIN(T)*(COS(F)-1.0)/A
```

```
      ALDEG=AL*180.0/PI

      TDEG=T*180.0/PI

      WRITE(6,200) ALDEG, TDEG, FDEG

     ENDIF

200   FORMAT(1H ,3F8.3)

 10 CONTINUE

     END
```

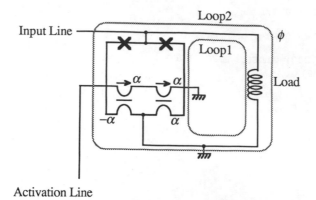

Fig.1   Scheme of basic QFP

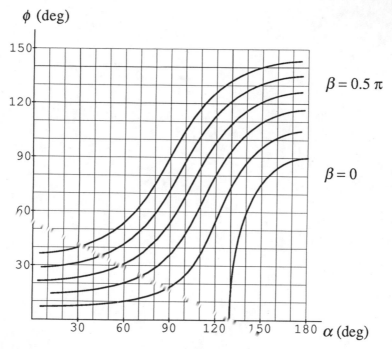

Graph 1   Activation of QFP:

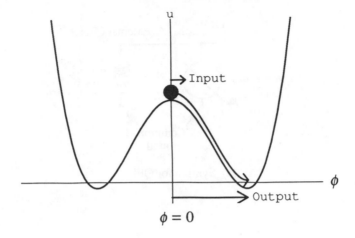

Fig. 2   Amplification Effect of QFP

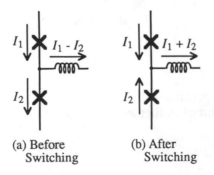

(a) Before
    Switching

(b) After
    Switching

Fig. 3   Current directions before and after switching

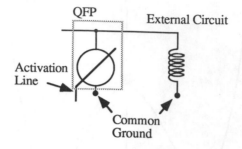

(a) Symbol for QFP

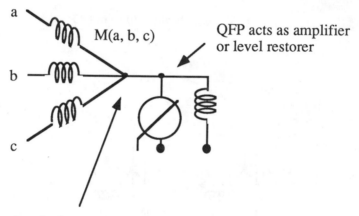

(b) 3-input Wired-Majority Gate

Fig. 4   QFP Majority Circuit

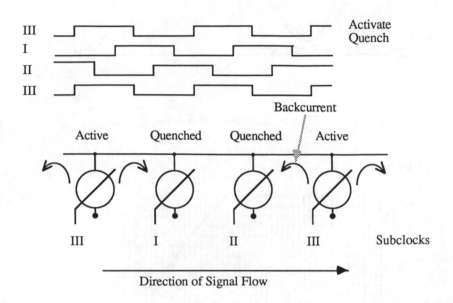

Fig. 5 3-phase Activation of QFPs

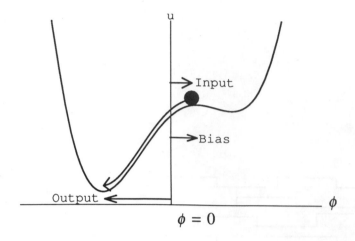

Fig. 6 Illustration of δI noise

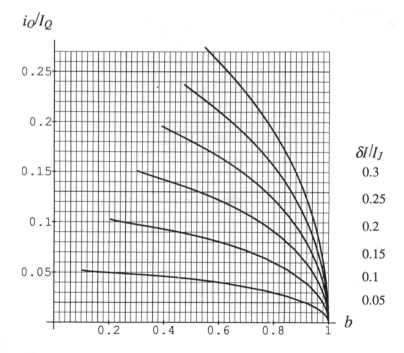

Graph 2 δI Characteristics

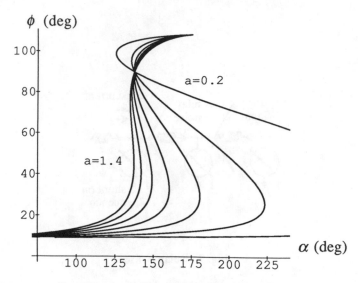

Graph 3   Activation characteristics of QFP
-- Effect of transformer inductance

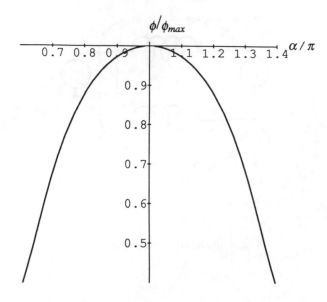

Graph 4   Effect of Activation Level on Output

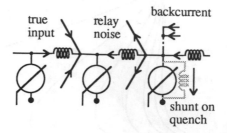

Fig. 7   Relay Noise

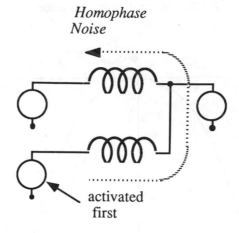

Fig. 8   Relayed Homophase Noise

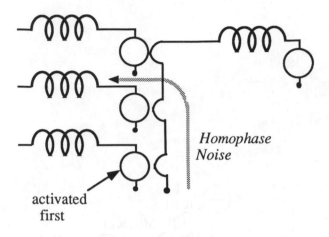

Fig. 9 Direct Homophase Noise

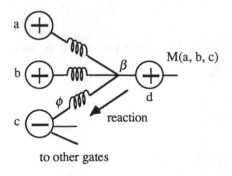

Fig. 10 Reaction hazard

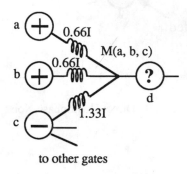

Fig. 11   Problem of Wired-Majority logic

Input
ϕ

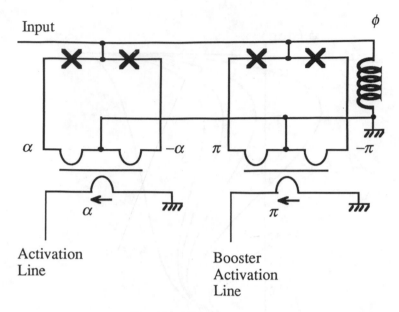

α $-\alpha$ π $-\pi$

α π

Activation
Line

Booster
Activation
Line

Fig. 12 QFP with Booster

i_O/I_Q

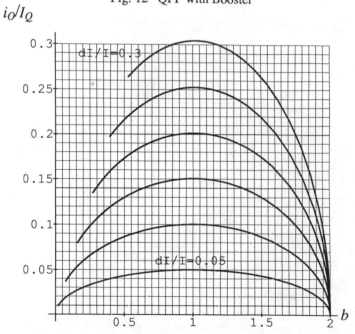

Graph 5 δI Noise characteristics of boostered-QFP

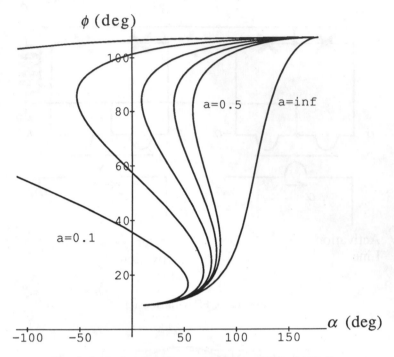

Graph 6   Activation Characteristics -- QFP with Puller

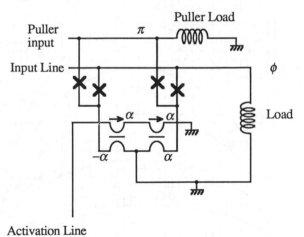

Fig. 13   Scheme of QFP with puller

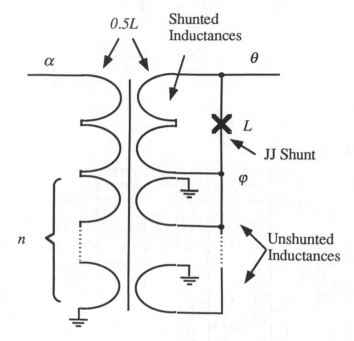

Fig. 14   Regulator

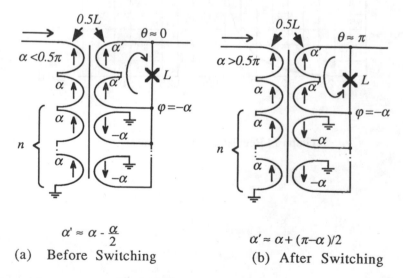

$$\alpha' \approx \alpha - \frac{\alpha}{2}$$

(a)   Before Switching

$$\alpha' \approx \alpha + (\pi - \alpha)/2$$

(b)   After Switching

Fig 15   Operation of Regulator

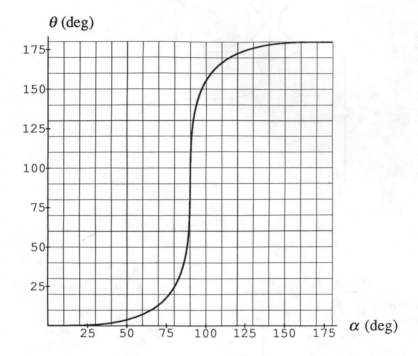

Graph 7   Regulator Characteristics

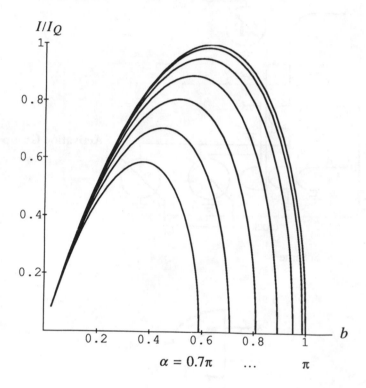

Graph 8   Output of QFP

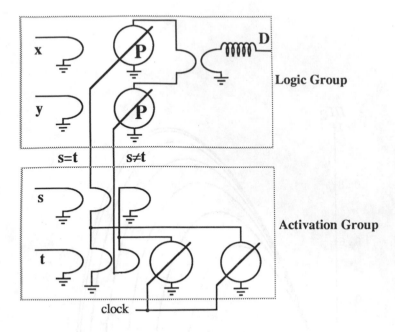

x

y

s=t   s≠t

s

t

clock

Logic Group

Activation Group

(a) Scheme

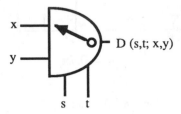

x

y

s   t

D (s,t; x,y)

(b) Symbol

Fig. 16 D-Gate

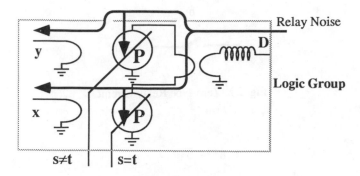

Fig. 17   Relay Noise in D-Gate

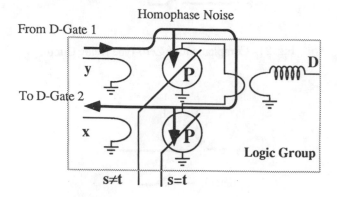

Fig. 18   Homophase Noise in D-Gate

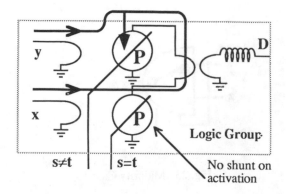

Fig. 19   Input Interaction

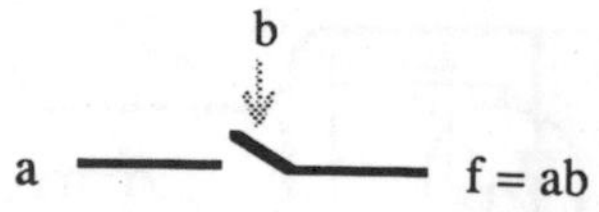

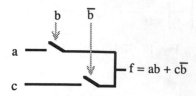

Fig. 20   Zero-type Relay Circuit

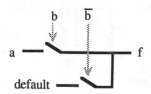

Fig. 21   Complementary Zero-type Relay Circuit

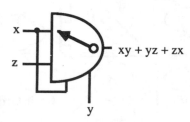

Fig. 22   Non-zero type Relay Switch

Fig. 23   Majority Gate

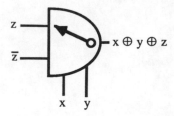

Fig. 24   Parity Gate

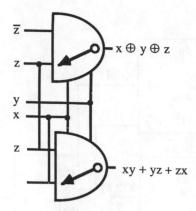

Fig. 25   Full Adder Gate

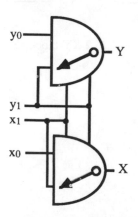

Fig. 26   Carry Lookahead Gate

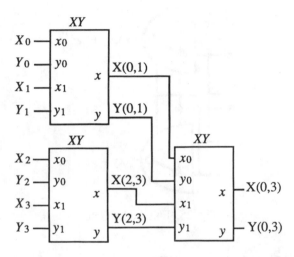

Fig. 27   2 XY-block stages

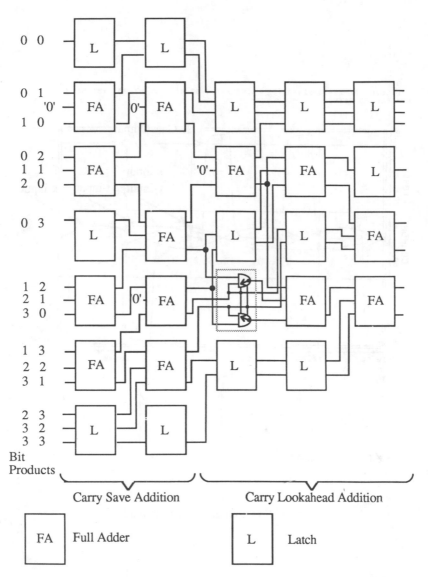

Bit
Products

Carry Save Addition   Carry Lookahead Addition

FA Full Adder   L Latch

Fig. 28 4x4 Pipelined Multiplier using D-Gates

178

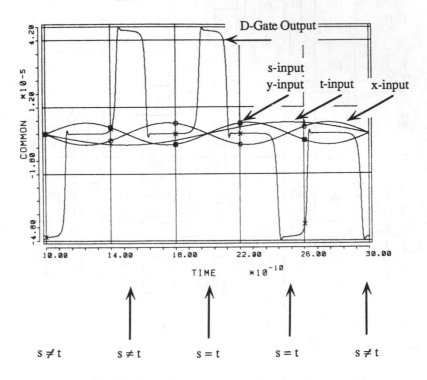

ALICE/M 02-27-90 14:35:32 DISPLAY(02-00-01) 03-07-90 13:56:59
*** FULL D-GATE

Plot 1   SPICE Output of D-Gate Simulation